JERSEY

Cover picture courtesy Jersey Tourism

Taking a break beside St Brelade's churchyard –
see Route 6, page 63

JERSEY CYCLES

~ *Exploring the Island by bike* ~

Arthur Lamy

SEAFLOWER BOOKS

Published in 2002 by
SEAFLOWER BOOKS

Seaflower Books is an imprint of
Ex Libris Press, to whom all enquiries
and correspondence should be addressed:

EX LIBRIS PRESS
1 The Shambles
Bradford on Avon
Wiltshire
BA15 1JS

Design and typesetting by Ex Libris Press
Printed in Britain by
Cromwell Press, Trowbridge, Wiltshire

ISBN 1 903341 11 6

CONTENTS

INTRODUCTION

One imagines Jersey, a small island of only 45 square miles, to be a cyclists' paradise. Sandy beaches, breathtaking views and sylvan valleys wait for you around every corner. But the difficulty for nearly everyone, visitor and local alike, is how to find this paradise without cycling miles of busy main roads or climbing too many hills. Furthermore, if locals do not know the quieter backroads, how will visitors fare?

In an effort to get more people to explore the island by bike, I have brought together 12 routes. All are loosely parish based and all meet the following criteria: they should bypass hills and main roads as much as possible, though in an island which rises from sea level to hills of almost 500 feet (153 metres) they are impossible to avoid, but are kept to a bare minimum. To cut down on any unnecessary cycling, all the routes start and finish in a car park, so that people can transport their bikes by car. Finally each route has to be sufficiently interesting to both motivate and entertain.

On average each circular route is 10 miles (16 km.) long. This distance should be easy enough for an inexperienced cyclist, whilst the closeness of one route to another will allow keener cyclists to join routes together. The routes to the starting points, for those who wish to cycle there, vary in length from 1.45 to 8.42 miles.

To make the 'Getting there' routes easy, I have used the cycle network which has routes numbered and signposted with small blue plaques. By following the text and the signs, one should be able to reach the start of each of our rides with the minimum of fuss using the quietest roads.

I originally created several of my routes before the award winning Green Lane network was set up, and I'm delighted to find that many of the roads that I had chosen are now designated 'Green Lanes'. This means that they are considered scenic, suitable for walkers, riders and cyclists and, best of all, have a 15mph speed limit.

Hopefully I have achieved most of my goals in this book and it will inspire both locals and visitors to explore some of Jersey's rich heritage and beautiful scenery by bike.

Arthur Lamy
St. Martin, Jersey
April 2002

JERSEY:
An Historical and Cultural Snapshot

Jersey became an island 8000 years ago, when rising sea levels cut it off from mainland France. Before then, the island's inhabitants were nomadic hunters following the huge herds of game as they migrated.

In 933 Jersey was annexed by William Longsword, Duke of Normandy. Norman rule had a great and far reaching effect on the island. Many of its present laws and customs stem from this period and though rarely heard spoken these days, our Jersey French patois is essentially old Norman French. The twelve parish churches were put up in Norman times, though the parishes themselves are a lot older. It is believed that they were established in the seventh or eighth century as feudal divisions for the apportionment of rates and tithes. Jersey was still under Norman rule when William the Conqueror, Duke of Normandy invaded England in 1066. This saw the island's ruler become the King of England. In 1204, King John of England lost his lands in France; Maine, Aquitaine and Normandy. This posed a problem for the noblemen living in Jersey, should they side with the King of France or the King of England? Most stayed loyal to the King of England, more through economic reasoning than anything else. Suddenly Jersey had become a frontier outpost of England, only 15 miles away from the coast of France.

In the intervening 500 years the French made many attempts to capture the island. Yet Jersey only came under French rule once, during the Wars of the Roses, when the island was sold by Queen Margaret of Anjou to the French for their support of the Lancastrian cause. This situation lasted seven years until 1468 when the island was captured by a Yorkist fleet under Sir Richard Harliston.

The last attempt to take Jersey for France was in 1781. This attack was led by Baron de Rullecourt, a veteran of the failed attack by the Prince of Nassau at St. Ouen's Bay two years earlier. De Rullecourt was very nearly successful. He managed to capture the island's governor, Moyse Corbett, and bluff him into believing he had a huge force already in control of the island. Corbett was taken in and signed the capitulation. Fortunately the alarm had been raised in the parishes, and a force of militia and regular troops was assembled on Westmount. Led by the young Major Francis Peirson, who was only 24 at the time, a successful attack was carried out on the French troops who occupied what is now called the Royal Square. Both De Rullecourt and Peirson were mortally wounded in the encounter.

Nearly 200 years passed before the island was to be occupied again. In July 1940, the island fell to the forces of Nazi Germany and remained under Nazi rule for the next five years.

Once in the island, the occupying forces immediately set about making the island impregnable. The results are impossible to overlook as the defences ring most of the coastline and can also be seen inland in the form of command bunkers and artillery positions.

From Napoleonic times we find the coast defended by Round Towers and shore batteries, while the ancient castle of Mont Orgueil harks back to the era of the bowman. Less obvious to the eye are the Iron Age castles of refuge like Le Catel at Grève de Lecq, Le Catel at Rozel and the almost now indiscernable Chastel Sedement at Trinity. In times of attack their simple earth walls would offer temporary shelter to the inhabitants.

In order to offer some resistance to these raids, an unpaid and homegrown defence force was established. Every man between the ages of 15 and 65 had to serve in the militia, which was a parish based fighting force. Every Sunday this force would be drilled and trained. The training ground would usually be near the parish church, until the parish arsenals were built in the early 1840s. After the First World War militia service was made voluntary, and after the Second World War the militia was disbanded altogether.

In a similiar way, Jersey's honorary police system also stems from the Middle Ages, being one of the earliest forms of policing in the world. Unlike the militia, service in the honorary police was entirely voluntary, which naturally ensures a dedicated and committed force. Since 1853, St. Helier the island's capital, has had a uniformed police force. But it was not until 1974 that the paid police force became islandwide. Today the honorary police still plays an important role in island policing, though the huge rise in population in the last fifty years has made it rather more impersonal than it used to be.

The head of the honorary police in each parish is the constable. He is voted in by his parishioners, and has the right to sit in the States, which is the island's parliament. In addition each parish has a number of deputies, depending on the size of the parish. Like the constable they sit for a three year term. Twelve senators, voted in on an islandwide mandate, complete the 53 members of the island's government. Senators sit in the States for a six year term, but half of them are elected every three years to ensure some continuity. This mix of individuals makes for a lively, but very democratic government. There are no party politics and politicians are voted in on personality as much as anything else.

The island is self governing, as it is neither a colony nor a part of the United Kingdom. It is what is referred to as a "Peculiar" or personal possession of the Crown. In fact we still refer to the monarch as our Duke, as to us, she is still our ruler the Duke of Normandy. Even today, whenever the Queen visits, it is normal practice for the seigneurs, or lords of the manor, to pay her homage just as they would have centuries ago. For example the seigneur of Trinity has to present the Queen with a brace of mallard, whilst the seigneur of Rozel has to act as butler to the Queen when she dines. These days though, the seigneur is often a wealthy tax exile rather than a local nobleman.

The generous tax laws in Jersey mean that the maximum rate of income tax is 20%. This offers an incentive to many to relocate to the island, providing that they meet the criteria for entry. The low rate of taxation and a stable government has also encouraged many banks and trust companies to move to Jersey. Since 1961, when the law restricting interest payments to a maximum of 5% was repealed, the door was opened for many financial institutions to set up in business in the island. Nowadays we have no fewer than 79 banks in Jersey, somewhere around £115.1 billion on deposit and £87.1 billion in investment funds. It comes as no surprise to discover that Jersey is a major financial centre.

At present, the island's position and low rate of tax favours the finance industry, but in the past Jersey has benefitted through its unique relationship with the Crown. For instance, any imports into England have never attracted any duty. In 1394 Richard II granted a charter to the Channel Islands which said that they were to be exempted from taxes and duties in English towns and ports.

This tariff free status did much to aid the island's exports and give them an advantage in the market place. As long ago as the 16th century Jersey was exporting woollen stockings. Mary, Queen of Scots is said to have worn a pair at her execution, perhaps they were a gift from her principle gaoler, Sir Amias Poulet, a former governor of Jersey. In the 18th.Century corn was brought in from the Baltic and ground in local mills before being shipped out to the colonies. And again in the 19th Century, when the Jersey cow came to the fore, and when the Jersey New Potato was discovered, a lack of tariffs made their promotion so much easier.

The advent of steam brought a regular packet service to the island, and Jersey became the most southerly point of the rail network. The benefits of this were twofold, an increase in visitors and a regular service to export island produce.

A new industry developed, tourism. The island's mild climate and closeness to Great Britain made the ideal holiday destination. In post-war years it was one of the principle engines of the economy, and like many other previous enterprises it was profitable for local business. Like farming, oyster fishing and the great civil works of the 19th Century, the hotel trade has relied heavily on imported labour. This, together with an English garrison stationed here until 1939, has meant that many temporary migrants have stayed and settled here.

The island's various industries and often her need for specialist labour has swelled the population, whilst her position so close to France has made the island a sanctuary for religious or political exiles. Today's islander could be the descendant of a Norman settler, a Huguenot refugee, an Irish labourer or a Breton farmworker.

It is these roots, together with a constant pulse of change and enterprise that has formed the island that we see today.

Getting Started: Equipment and Advice

A keen cyclist will always say that any bicycle is better than none, but a correctly fitting, well maintained bike is the best of all.

The best bike will have powerful brakes and gears low enough to tackle any hill that presents itself. All this sounds promising, but you'll notice that I always suggest walking if you feel any hill is uncomfortable, in either direction. One of the attractions of cycling is the opportunity to see, smell and hear so much that the motorist leaves behind. Therefore a slower pace, on occasion, does no harm at all.

If you are a newcomer to cycling, or if you prefer the easiest option, a bike with three rings on the front chainset will ensure that hills do not present a problem. Do not be alarmed by the number of gears cycles have because these days all bikes have gears which click into place, making it impossible to miss a gear. Furthermore it is not neccessary to start off in the lowest gear, on an average ride one might use four or five different ratios, so the rider is not constantly changing gears.

Both hybrid and mountain bikes have cantilever type brakes which offer excellent stopping power, and also a range of extra low gears. Remember though that the wide knobbly tyres of a mountain bike can make road cycling heavy going. Often changing the tyres to something smoother and narrower will overcome this.

Bicycles, like clothes, come in different sizes and it is important that your bike fits you correctly. As a rough guide the correct frame size should allow you to put your heel on the pedal, when the pedal crank is at it's lowest and in line with the seat tube. In this position your leg should be almost straight. When you achieve this, there should be 4 or 5 inches of seat post showing. If the reach to the handlebars is correct, your arms and torso should form an approximate right angle. Needless to say comfort is the main criterion, and a competant cycle shop will be able to assist you to find the right bike or adjust your own.

One or two accessories may help you enjoy your cycling; every route in this book has a number of mileage checks to ensure that you are on the right road, so an inexpensive cycle computer will help with this. If you are planning to carry any weight a rear carrier is a lot less tiring than a rucksack, particularly on a hot day. Also a small pannier bag or handlebar bag will allow you to carry your valuables around with you if you leave the bike. On most routes there is an opportunity to buy food and drink, but a water bottle may fill the gaps in between.

Nearly every ride has a number of far reaching views so a pair of binoculars and a small compass may add to your enjoyment. Finally don't forget your lock and your helmet.

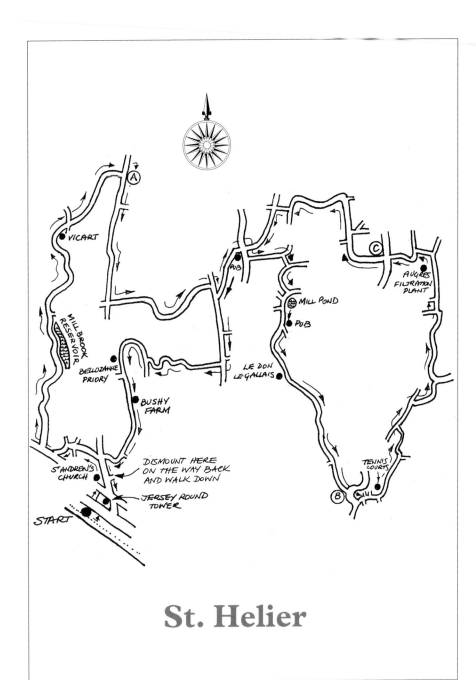

VICART

MILL BROOK RESERVOIR

BELLOZANNE PRIORY

BUSHY FARM

ST ANDREN'S CHURCH

DISMOUNT HERE ON THE WAY BACK AND WALK DOWN

JERSEY ROUND TOWER

START

Ⓐ

PUB

MILL POND

PUB

LE DON LE GALLAIS

Ⓒ

AUGRES FILTRATION PLANT

TENNIS COURTS

Ⓑ

St. Helier

St. Helier

A Tale of Five Valleys

At first, St. Helier may seem an odd choice for a pleasant cycle ride, but its boundaries extend sufficiently into the countryside to allow us a glimpse of some beautiful scenery. With its western and eastern limits defined by the streams that run through Waterworks Valley and Grand Vaux, and with three more valleys in between, our route is punctuated by several quite steep climbs and descents. As usual I suggest walking whenever you want to, as these routes are intended to be enjoyable and in no way a physical challenge.

Getting there: Approximate distance 1.45 miles; 2.33 km.

Leave **Liberation Square** and using the crossing, cross over the dual carriageway to reach the harbour. Here, turn right and head west towards the underpass. Cycling parallel to the road, climb the rise and, using care, cross the two roads that lead to the Elizabeth Terminal.

Follow the gravel track, crossing the car park sliproad, and soon we reach granite paving, where the cycle track is defined by a single white line running alongside the old sea wall.

When the wall finishes the track is marked by parallel white lines. Do not forget that we share the promenade with pedestrians, roller bladers and other cyclists, so exercise caution.

As a mileage check, we pass the **Grand Hotel** in 0.55 miles; 0.89 km., and we should reach our starting point, the layby immediately after the first set of traffic lights, at **First Tower**, in 1.45 miles; 2.33km.

The Route: Approximate distance 11.10 miles; 17.86 km.

Leave the car park and cycle towards St. Helier for a short distance. On reaching the **Victoria Avenue** crossing dismount and using the lights, cross over. Once we are across, turn left and walk along the pavement, turning right to go between the Round Tower and the buildings on the left. Use the crossing to cross this road and then bear right to the bottom of the hill.

Cycle up the hill, avoiding a right turn. We pass the church and park of St. Andrew on the left. **St. Andrew's Church** was built in 1926 to replace the chapel of St. Andrew, the seamen's mission, that had stood on the Esplanade since 1854. Ascend a little further to leave **Mont Cochon** and turn left into **Rue de Trachy**.

Freewheel past an old Jersey farmhouse with its typical double arched gates. Cross through a small crossroads, the road bends left and descends further. At the yellow line at the end of Rue de Trachy, dismount and walk along the pavement on the right. This will save us the problem of entering and exiting a very busy road to gain ten yards. Walk past the church and the shops, and turn right into **Le Chemin des Moulins**. For the next mile or so we will be cycling up one of the prettiest valleys in the island.

Soon we arrive at **Millbrook Reservoir**, built in 1895. This was the first reservoir built in the island. From here water was piped to St. Helier, where the street hand pumps could not provide sufficient water for the expanding population. Two more reservoirs were built further up the valley; Dannemarche in 1909, and Handois in 1932.

Before the reservoirs arrived, the valley floor was lined by watermills. The stream that flows through this valley is the most powerful in the island, falling nearly 400 feet in three miles. It is not surprising to discover that it drove six watermills, which included a paper mill and a mill that crushed sugar cane. Milling was a profitable business. Corn was brought in directly from Russia, ground in local mills and then shipped out to the colonies, where it could be landed free of duty. However, with the advent of steam power, the water driven mill had had its day.

Continue up the valley, missing a hill on the right. Further on we pass a lone white building at **Vicart**. Just afterwards the road bends left, and we need to bear right up the hill ahead, **Mont du Bu de la Rue**. At the yellow line at the end of Mont du Bu de la Rue (**A**), we have cycled 2.54 miles; 4.09 km. Here we turn right on to Mont Cochon again and head south. Miss a lane on the left and, as we freewheel along, we can see the spire of St. Lawrence Church and the tower of the Parish Hall, across the valley to our right.

The name Mont Cochon has nothing to do with pigs, despite a certain Matthieu Le Porcq being vingtenier for the area at the beginning of the eighteenth century. Rather it was the name of a family living in the vicinity.

After a slight kink in the road, take the next left into the Green Lane, **Fern Valley**. The road drops away quite steeply here, so be ready with your brakes. This charming lane meanders along the valley floor, bordered along most of its length by National Trust woodland, before it rises again, finally exiting at the junction with **La Grande Route de Mont à L'Abbé**.

Turn left here into **La Rue de Maupertuis**. We will use this lane again, going in the opposite direction, later on in our ride.

When we reach the main road at the end of Rue de Maupertuis turn right, but exercise caution as the road is usually very busy. After ten yards or so, turn left into **Rue des Arbres**. The road descends as we turn right into a very steep lane that leads us to the top of **Vallée des Vaux**. At the bottom of the hill, turn right following *Route 5* and, at the next yellow line, turn right to follow

Above: Old Tractor in Fern Valley

Left: Babbling brook in Vallée des Vaux

the valley. The pond on the left supports a flock of geese and ducks, but it was originally the millpond supplying water to power the wheel at Nicolle Mill, which is the next building along on the left, nowadays a pub.

Crest the rise and pass two lanes on the right. From this point it is possible to freewheel for over half a mile, and we do not have to turn a pedal until we reach the outskirts of the town. Pass a NO ENTRY on the left and freewheel on past a sign warning of 15 mph radar checks. Much of the wooded land on the side of the valley is owned by the National Trust for Jersey. In fact the first plot of land owned by the Trust can be found on the right, opposite a group of houses. This is **Le Don Carlysle Le Gallais**. Since then the Trust has accumulated over 120 properties, thus preserving the island's natural beauty.

The stream burbles away on our left as we make for the outskirts of St. Helier. We pass a supermarket, and at the end of Vallée des Vaux at the yellow line (**B**) we have covered 5.83 miles; 9.38 km. Here turn right and descend for a few yards before turning left into **Trinity Road**. Pass a turning on the right and then two on the left and we find ourselves in **Les Vaux New Road**. Pass another right turn and cycle past the tennis courts.

Cycle along the valley, passing a hill that enters on the right and, after a short distance, another hill that comes in on the left. When the road forks, bear right continuing on *Route 7*. The road swings left and we arrive at another fork, where we bear left into **Les Ruisseaux**. As we climb, we leave the outskirts and head back into the country. At the top of the hill the road bends left and becomes **Oaklands Lane**. We immediately turn right into a narrow lane and continue on, passing a turn on the left some way up.

The lane rises and we pass **Augres Filtration Plant** on the left. Soon after, turn left and then left again at the yellow line. The lane bends to the right and we arrive at a crossroads (**C**). We have covered 7.69 miles; 12.38km. so far. Using care, cross over from **Rue de la Croiserie** into **Rue de la Garenne**. Cycle on and follow the lane as it bends right, before passing a lane on the left and then two lanes on the right further on. The road dips and turns to the left, as it skirts **Le Douet**. It descends further between two expanses of water. The stream which feeds these two is the one that accompanied us as we sped down Vallée des Vaux, and which has its humble beginnings in St. John.

The road rises again and bends to the left. Instead of going straight ahead, turn right into **Rue de Becquet Vincent** and then left at the crossroads into **La Rue du Haute de l'Orme**. When we arrive at the St. John's Main Road again, go carefully across the junction to retrace our steps along Rue de Maupertuis.

Coast down this lane as it bears left into La Grande Route de Mont à L'Abbé. Once in La Grande Route de Mont à L'Abbé, freewheel on past a small lane on the left and, after the road rises, miss another left and turn right into **Rue Fliquet**. This lane dives left and right as it descends into **Bellozanne Valley** and, as the lane drops away very suddenly, I would recommend walking if you are at all unsure about your riding ability.

At the yellow line at the end of Rue Fliquet bear right and follow the lane as it climbs out of this last valley. As this hill is particularly steep, I would suggest walking. As we climb it is hard to believe that we are still in Jersey's capital, St. Helier. At the summit stands a perfect example of traditional local architecture, **Bellozanne Priory**.

Despite the name, this house has no connection with the Church, other than standing in the fief which once belonged to the Abbey of Saint Marie de Bellozanne in Normandy.

Once past the Priory, a good stretch of flat road lies ahead. Pass a lane on the left and continue on into **La Ruelle Vaucluse**. The tall striped chimney of the refuse incinerator dominates the horizon on the left.

Cycling further up the lane we discover **Bushy Farm**, home of the Jersey Royal potato.

> It was at Bushy Farm, in 1880, that Hugh de la Haye was given, as a joke, a huge potato with sixteen shoots sprouting from it. He cut the potato into sixteen pieces and planted them on his fertile south-facing slopes in the valley below us. One of the pieces produced a particularly fine early potato, and it is from this that today's crop is derived.

Soon we arrive at the end of this stretch of road but, before it swoops away to the right, stop and admire a rather unusual aspect of St. Aubin's Bay. Freewheel down this final hill, but be ready to brake at the yellow line that appears quite suddenly after the bend.

At the end of La Ruelle Vaucluse turn left and return down Mont Cochon. When we reach the NO ENTRY, halfway down, it is quicker to dismount and walk to the bottom than to cycle an alternative route. At the bottom we retrace our footsteps back to the start.

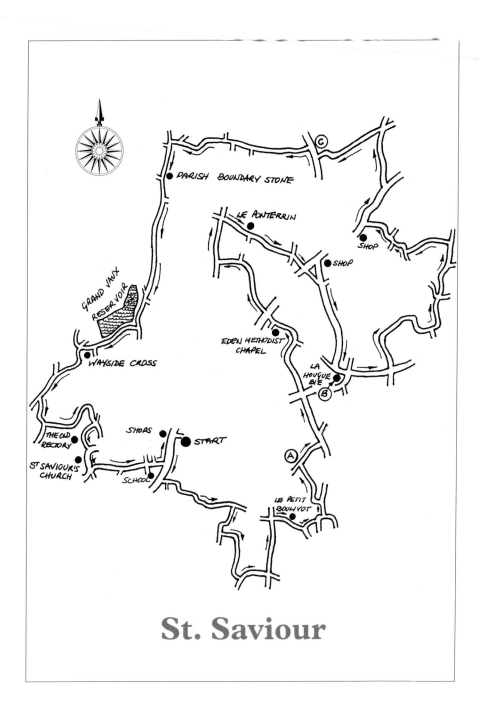

St. Saviour

St. Saviour
Home to the Jersey Lily

Like St. Clement, St. Saviour is a parish which has seen much growth in population and subsequent building in the last fifty years. In fact its population has more than trebled since the 1901 census. Despite all this, it is nevertheless possible to enjoy a ride in a parish which is inherently rural.

I was surprised to discover that two of the ancient engines of the economy – apple orchards and sheep farming – could be still found in the parish, albeit on a much smaller scale than in previous times.

Before we set off, I must mention that St. Saviour has more than its fair share of school traffic, so it is probably wise to plan your tour between school rush hours.

Getting there: Approximate distance 2.20 miles; 3.54 km.

Leave **Liberation Square** and head towards the dual carriageway between the harbour and the square. If the road is busy, wait until the traffic lights at the crossing stop the traffic, then turn left and take the middle lane. This will take us to the right of the bus station and through the tunnel which runs under Fort Regent.

As we approach the end of the tunnel bear right and go straight through the roundabout. A slight slope will take us through two junctions, and we will arrive at a set of traffic lights with 0.6 miles; 0.97 km. cycled.

Turn left at these traffic lights and carry on towards another set of traffic lights ahead. Approaching these, use the middle lane which will put us in the right-hand lane at the lights. Turn right here and cycle through another set of lights. Bearing slightly left continue up the hill. The hill bends left as it rises.

Follow this hill as it passes a school on the left, **Victoria College**, with a playing field opposite. We pass another school, **Jersey College for Girls**, a little further on. Go through a small crossroads, followed by a larger and busier crossroads. Here our mileometer should read 1.7 miles; 2.74 km.

Continuing on, we pass a wayside cross followed almost immediately by **St. Saviour's Primary School**. Just after the school miss a left turning and take the second right into a car park, which is situated across the road from a row of shops. The blue car park sign should be easy to spot as we draw near.

The Route: Approximate distance 11 miles; 17.7 km.

Our starting point is the small car park opposite the shops at **Bagatelle Parade**, just before the roundabout at Five Oaks. It is possible to park here for an hour, though the distance from St.Helier is so short that it may be easier to cycle from town. On Sundays, it is possible to park here all day.

From this starting point, make your way back to the main road, opposite the shops and turn left. After passing St.Saviour's Primary School on the right, turn left into **Rue de La Retraite**. Head towards the triple arches of **Beau Desert** at the end of the road.

The road flicks right and left and descends into **Swiss Valley**. A substantial bridge crosses the valley stream, and after winding right and left, a stiff climb takes us out of the valley. When the road levels out turn right into **La Freminierie**. The sea comes into view, the Demi des Pas beacon and the rocks at Greve D'Azette can be seen almost straight ahead.

Just before the road begins to descend, turn left into **Rue des Champs**. We are soon able to enjoy a spirited freewheel almost down to sea level. After a bend in the road we arrive at a yellow line where we turn left. Once past the hotel on the left, look to your right and we see a young apple orchard.

> Cider is still made in the island, though on a very small scale. Strict rules regarding production and the lack of sufficient apples prevent cider-making on a commercial basis, unlike two hundred years ago when cider and cider apples were the principle export, and St.Saviour was the principle parish for their cultivation.

At the crossroads, turn left into **Rue de Tapon**. We climb gently as we pass **Le Tapon Farm** on our right. At the next crossroads, take a right into **Le Boulivot de Bas**. An easy freewheel allows us to catch our breath, though this may be arrested again by **Le Petit Boulivot**, which is a classic pre-1700 dwelling. The stone set into the wall marks the border between Grouville and St. Saviour. When the road divides, bear left and then turn left at the T-junction. The road bends to the right and at the next yellow line turn left again.

For a short distance we follow *Route 8* until we take a left into a lane which sees little traffic, borne out by the weeds growing in the middle of the tarmac. At the end of this lane turn right into **Rue de Paradis (A)**, our mileometer should read 2.3 miles; 3.70 km..

Turn left at the yellow line and continue on, missing a right turn. As we draw up to the crossroads at the end of **Rue de la Parade**, look over to your right. The large copse of trees in the distance hides the neolithic tomb of La Hougue Bie, one of the finest in Western Europe, which we will visit later. Cross over this main road into **Rue de la Commune**. After the playing field on the left, the profusion of vegetation traces the run of a stream, which is also indicated by an open culvert alongside the road.

Quite a rare sight in these times of litigation. Miss a right, and follow *Route 3* towards **Victoria Village**.

Before the next junction we pass **Eden Methodist Chapel**, built in 1833.

Methodism came to Jersey by quite a tortuous route. It was brought here by two young Jerseymen, Pierre Le Sueur and Jean Tentin. They had discovered this new religion whilst engaged in the cod fishing industry, off the Gaspé Coast of Canada. This was an industry that involved many local men, both as fishermen and as merchants. Many local fortunes were made in the Cod Trade.

At the junction with the main road, leave **Rue des Pigneaux**, and being careful, cross over into **Fosse a L'Ecrivain**, again following *Route 3*. The road rises and falls as we cross a water meadow. Miss a right and proceed slightly uphill to a T-junction. Here turn right into **Rue du Chateau Clairval**. Notice the granite wall of the football pitch, beautifully dressed granite with darker stone set into it to form two diamond shapes.

Turn right at the next crossroads. This lane descends and at the bottom, opposite a lane on the right, stop to admire the façade of an old farmstead. The classic twin entrance arches may be seen, the smaller pedestrian entrance on the left has now become a window of the current dwelling. If we carry on a little further up this lane, we will see the original house, **Le Ponterrin**, at the rear. This building dates from the early 16th.century, and it is almost untouched by time. The building on the roadside was originally the outbuildings of Le Ponterrin.

Continue up a slight ascent, pass through a crossroads and at the next crossroads, where **Rue du Ponterrin** ends, cross over the main road and then turn right at the yellow line.

We soon see the highlight of our ride in the distance amongst the trees, **La Hougue Bie**. By the time we reach La Hougue Bie, our mileometer should read almost 5 miles; 8.05 km. (**B**).

La Hougue Bie is an exceptional example of a neolithic tomb. Unlike many dolmens, it still retains the protective mound of stone and earth around it. Within the grounds we will also find an archaeology and geology museum, and a German command bunker, now a museum dedicated to the slave workers brought to the islands during the Second World War. Though there is no café, it is possible to buy light refreshments.

Left: La Hougue Bie, Chapel of Notre Dame de la Clarté;
Right: The entrance to the Neolithic Tomb

On leaving La Hougue Bie turn right, and continue straight on through the crossroads adjacent to the site. We can freewheel to the next turning, which is first left into **Rue de la Hambie**. The lane bends to the right and then meanders right and left before passing a lane on the right. If we look to our right we will see a square cream-coloured building, the old eastern telephone exchange. Here a group of ladies would connect your calls manually, before the advent of automatic dialling.

Another sharp left-hand bend takes us under a canopy of trees, and we can freewheel down to the yellow line, passing a Green Lane sign on the way. Cross over this tiny crossroads and climb out of the shallow valley. The road levels out and gets unusually wide for a country lane. Avoid a right turn but take the next left soon after the lane begins to dip. Follow this lane to a T junction, where we turn right. The lane twists left and right and descends. Proceed straight through and up a slight incline, passing another Green Lane sign. A magnificent collection of greenhouses lines this short stretch of road.

At the junction at the end of **Chasse du Mourin** turn right onto the St. Martin's main road. Travel along the main road for a short distance and take the first left. When we reach a crossroads, take a left into **Rue des Cabarettes**. This lane has a number of attractive granite houses along its length. Look out for a diagonal line in the tarmac in the S bend at the end of this lane – this marks the border between St. Martin and St. Saviour. Another clue to the change of parish can be found when we reach the yellow line, because the lane has now become **Rue de Sacrement**. By now we have covered 7.5 miles; 12.07 km. (**C**). Turn right here and head north for a few yards before turning left into **Rue du Pont**. The tall metal tower on the right is a silo for storing cattle feed. Continue ahead, missing two turnings on the left and one on the right. The lane twists left and right and after passing a lane on the right we arrive at a yellow line.

Here we turn left into **La Rue de la Boucterie**. Miss a right and head straight on. We are now on *Route 7*, heading south towards our starting point. Just after an old shop, look on the tarmac for the tell-tale line, the tablet on the wall should give you a good clue. Continue on *Route 7*, passing a left turn. Soon the road will descend steeply into **Grand Vaux Valley**, but just before it does, take a look over to your right. In the distance we see the town of St. Helier and the sea, framed on either side by the valley walls.

Using caution, freewheel down this steep hill. On reaching the valley floor, follow the road as it sweeps along beside the reservoir, passing the St. Saviour's Millennium Stone, until we reach a wayside cross at the foot of **Deloraine Road**. This cross was put up in 1928 by Athelstan Riley, the Seigneur of Trinity, as a memorial to his daughter-in-law, who was killed here in a riding accident.

Press on through the valley, past a modern housing estate built quite recently to replace the high rise blocks which were there since the sixties.

Cycle past two right turnings and take the first left into **Langley Park**. The hill rises fairly gently and after a bend becomes **Langley Avenue**. In a few yards we arrive at an S-bend. Using great care, turn right into a narrow lane. Freewheel down this lane, and after a slight bend to the left we discover a property on the right called **The Old Rectory**.

This was the birthplace of the world-renowned beauty Lillie Langtry. Her father was William Corbet Le Breton, Rector of St. Saviour and Dean of Jersey. Born in 1853, Lillie was christened Emilie Charlotte Le Breton, and was the only girl in a family of seven children.

Her career and lifestyle would be exceptional by today's standards, but by Victorian standards it was outrageous. At twenty she married Edward Langtry, the son of a wealthy Belfast shipowner. She became the mistress of the Prince of Wales, and in 1881 she had a daughter by Prince Louis of Battenburg. She became an American citizen, toured the world as an actress, appearing at the opening of the Jersey Opera House in "The Degenerates", a play written for her by Sidney Grundy. She married her second husband Hugo de Bathe, a gentleman some nineteen years her junior, in 1899. In 1907 she was the first woman to break the bank at Monte Carlo. Lillie died in Monaco in 1929, and was laid to rest in St.Saviour's churchyard as was her wish.

If we cycle on, we soon reach the junction with the main hill out of St.Helier. Here, we can enter the churchyard and following the path on the right we will easily find Lillie's last resting place.

Leave the church and ride down the hill past St.Saviour's Parish Hall. Immediately after the Parish Hall turn left into **Patier Road**. Cycle up this gentle incline, passing through a crossroads and passing the Primary School again. At the T junction turn left to regain our starting point.

St. Lawrence
Heritage heartland

St.Lawrence encapsulates so much that is rural in the island. In the quiet, tree lined lanes of the parish, it is so peaceful that you could forget where you are.

Getting there*: Approximate distance 2.6 miles; 4.18 km.*

Leave **Liberation Square** and, using the crossing, cross the dual carriageway to reach the harbour. Once on the quayside, turn right and head west towards the underpass. Cycle parallel to the road. After the pavement rises, using care, cross the two roads that lead to the Elizabeth Terminal.

Once over the two roads, we cycle on a rough gravel path which crosses the car park sliproad. Soon the path becomes granite paving when we reach the old sea wall. Here the cycle track is marked by a single white line running parallel to the wall. As the sea wall ends, the route becomes marked by two white lines. The promenade is used by pedestrians, roller bladers and even a motorised train, so be cautious and ready with your bell.

The track continues on to St. Aubin, the village at the end of the bay. As a guide to mileage, we will pass the Jersey Round Tower at **First Tower** in 1.31 miles; 2.11 km., the **Old Station Café** in 1.75 miles; 2.82 km. and the burger bar at the end of Victoria Avenue in 2.12 miles; 3.41 km.

We reach our starting point for today's ride, the small car park with the white railings, in 2.57 miles; 4.14 km. It is simple to find, as it lies between the cycle track and the road. At the far end is a phone box and on the corner is a cycle *Route 4* sign.

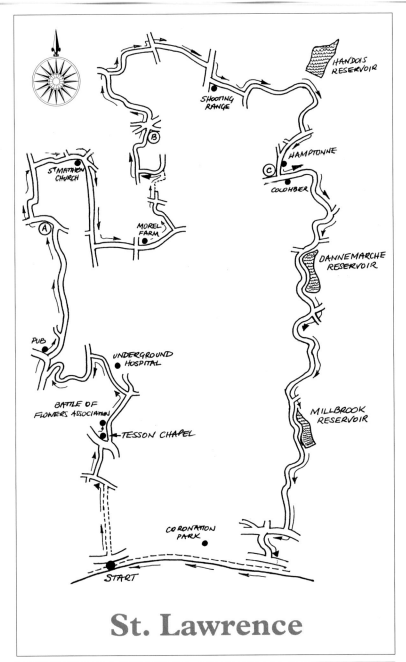

St. Lawrence

The Route: Approximate distance 10.7 miles; 17.22 km.

Our ride starts in the small car park that lies between the main road and the seaside cycle track, just over half way along the Bel Royal to Beaumont road.

Leave the car park and cross the road, using the crossing. Cycle up the gravel track that is a perquage path.

> Centuries ago, criminals could seek santuary in a church and, using a perquage path they could escape the island by boat without being arrested. This particular perquage was the gateway to freedom for people fleeing from St.Lawrence Parish Church, and it is also thought to be have been used by people fleeing St.John and St.Mary.

When the path reaches the road turn left and then immediately right into **Rue du Moulin**. Ride up to the junction with the valley road. Here turn right and then left by **Tesson Chapel**, to cycle up **La Rue de Pres Sorsoleil**. Pass the headquarters of the Battle of Flowers Association and take the first left into **Mont du Rocher**, a Green Lane. This is quite a steep hill, so dismount and walk.

> Halfway up we overlook the German Underground Hospital, a large tunnel entrance with a Red Cross above it. These tunnels were originally planned as an artillery barracks and storage facility. With 130 feet of rock above it, it makes an ideal place for storing munitions. Construction started in September 1941, and yet it was not completed at the end of the war. Despite this, enough had been done to allow it to function fully as a hospital. By the end of 1944, 600 beds, an operating theatre, staff quarters, kitchens, air conditioning and central heating were all in place. It was the changing tide of the war that prompted the decision to convert the tunnels into a hospital. Fortunately the island never came under direct attack and the hospital was never used.

German Tunnel: Vehicle entrance (left); Pedestrian entrance (right)

Climb a little further and at the T-junction turn left into **Les Gelettes**. The lane bends right and begins to descend into St. Peter's Valley. As it steepens, it twists its way through trees, before emerging on the valley road. Turn right here, and head towards the pub, where we bear right up **Route de L'Aleval**.

> Before 1966 this was a gravel track going up to the German tunnels on the left. The three entrances that we see are all part of the same complex. The two larger entrances, the last one that we pass is blocked up now, were to allow vehicles to enter and exit quickly. Whilst the small one in the middle was solely for pedestrians. Pass a Green Lane on the left as we ascend. When we reach the yellow line at the top of the hill (**A**), we have cycled 2.49 miles; 4.01 km.

Here, turn left into **Rue de Petit Aleval** and then right into **Rue des Aix**. The lane bends right and left and we take the next right into **Rue Bechervaise**. Pass a lane on the left and the road sweeps right between St. Matthew's Church and a huge sinister building which seems to have been a convent, the moulding high on the wall says "Immaculate Conception".

Cycle past the church and, avoiding the NO ENTRY and the Green Lane on the left, bear right into **Rue de la Ville au Bas**. We can freewheel back towards the heart of the parish, passing some classic local architecture as we do so. Miss a right and take the next left into **Rue de la Fontaine de St. Martin**. At the crossroads go straight over. Shortly, we pass **Morel Farm**.

This property belongs to the National Trust for Jersey and it is an exceptional example of a traditional farmstead. It has the usual double arched gates, in this case the gates are somewhat unusual in that they revolve in stone sockets and have no hinges. The farmhouse has pantiles on the roof, although it was previously thatched. Notice the small ledges on the chimneys, legend has it that these were resting places for the fairies, but they are really there to stop rain running between the chimney and the thatch.

Leave Morel Farm and descend the lane. Before reaching the valley floor, turn left and climb **Mont Isaac**. The lane meanders as we climb. At the yellow line at the top cross straight over into a very narrow Green Lane. This little lane gets narrower as it skirts behind a granite property then, after turning left for a few yards, it meets the highway in a bend. Here turn left and head towards the spire of St.Matthew's Church on the horizon. At the end of **Ruette D'Avranches**, where the Green Lane ends, turn right. Follow this lane as it approaches a small hamlet. This area is called Six Roads for obvious reasons. When we arrive at the yellow line at the end of **La Rue Rouge Cul** (**B**), we have cycled 4.84 miles; 7.79 km. Go across the yellow line and bear slightly left into **Les Chanolles des Six Rues**.

We can freewheel for a short distance after the road bends left. Cycle through a wide S bend and, after the road bends right, we approach a left-hand bend. Here, using care, turn right into **La Rue des Varvots**. Follow this lane as it meanders and descends, only to rise again and arrive at a T-junction. Turn left and immediately right into **La Rue de la Golarde**. Continue on, up to the yellow line at the main road, and turn right. After 200 yards turn left into **La Fraide Rue**. Pass the shooting range on the right and proceed on to the next junction, where we turn left into **La Rue es Gazeaux**. This lane leads us down to the head of **Handois Reservoir**.

The lane runs parallel to a stream that has escaped the reservoir. Following the stream we weave our way through this tiny valley. At the next yellow line, turn right and climb **La Rue de Bas**. As we cycle up avoid the lane on the right and, at the yellow line at the top, turn left. The road dips and we draw level with **Hamptonne**, the living farm museum, on the left.

Hamptonne is another jewel of Jersey's heritage which, fortunately, was purchased by the National Trust for Jersey in 1987, with assistance from the States of Jersey. As well as having 17th, 18th and 19th century buildings on the site, the farm is also of some historical importance. Lauren Hamptonne, who bought the property in 1637, was a friend of Charles II. In fact it was he who proclaimed Charles II king in the Royal Square, after hearing of Charles I's execution. In 1649, Charles granted Letters Patente to the property, which means that the property could never be divided, and the owners could attend the Assize d'Heritage with the seigneurs. Due to this, the property is also often known as La Patente, and the road it stands in is called Rue de la Patente. If we stop to visit, we can lock our bikes to the rings set in the wall. They are really for tethering cows, but serve equally well for bikes.

Leave Hamptonne and cycle up to the yellow line at the end of **Rue de la Patente**. By now we have cycled 7.12 miles; 11.46 km. (**C**).

Turn left into **Chemin du Moulin**. Before going too far, take a moment to inspect the square building on the right.

This is a colombier. In it would live hundreds of pigeons. This particular colombier is unusual in two respects; firstly it is one of only two square colombiers in the island and secondly, when it was built in 1445, the owner of the land was not a seigneur. Only seigneurs or lords of the manor had the right to have a colombier. As we can deduce from the stone above the entrance, the colombier was rebuilt in 1674 by Lauren Hamptonne's son Edouard.

Regain the road and begin a brisk freewheel through Waterworks Valley. Miss a hill on the left, when the road bends right, and continue past another hill on the left and then a lane on the right. The reservoir on our left is **Dannemarche Reservoir**, built in 1909. Coast past as the road bends. At the next bend follow the road around to the right, avoiding two lanes on the left.

We will have lost most of our momentum by the time we pass the steep hill on the left and arrive at the last reservoir. This is **Millbrook Reservoir**, the first catchment area built in Jersey.

When the valley road meets the main road, turn right and cycle up the slight incline to take the first left into **La Rue du Galet**. Freewheel down, but before reaching the lights, dismount and walk along the pavement, tracing *Route 2*, to reach the pedestrian crossing. Using the crossing, cross **Victoria Avenue** and remount when we get to the cycle track. Once there turn right to head back to our starting point.

The park which lies beyond the dual carriageway on the right is **Coronation Park**.

> This magnificent park was a gift to the island from Florence Boot, Lady Trent, wife of Jesse Boot the founder of Boots the Chemist. She also had the small church of St.Matthew, just at the side of the park, refurbished in memory of her husband. To carry out the work Florence Boot engaged René Lalique, a French artist famous for his work using glass, to make the church furniture. Inside, amongst other things, we will find a glass altar and a glass font.

Cycle on along the track to get back to our starting point.

St. Clement

A panoramic parish

St. Clement is the island's smallest parish having an area of only 1.6 square miles, despite this it is the second most densely populated parish after St. Helier, the island's capital.

Our starting point is Green Island car park. Green Island or La Motte, as it is correctly known, is the small island just to our right as we look out to sea. It has suffered erosion from the sea, but in the past it was attached to land, and was used as a prehistoric burial site.

Getting there: Approximate distance 2.7 miles; 4.35 km.

Leave Jersey Tourism, and head north into town, going up **Conway Street**, which borders the **Pomme D'Or Hotel** on its left-hand side. Go up Conway Street and take the second right into **Bond Street**. We pass the railings of the **Town Church** on our left, at the junction go straight over into **Pier Road**, which rises ahead in front of us.

When the road flattens out, we pass a multi-storey car park on the left. Just after the car park take a left into a road which comes in at an angle. Climb a little more, and at the summit follow the road round to the left, the road then narrows and bends to the right as it goes under some trees.

At the yellow line, turn left and descend the hill into **Havre des Pas**. Continue on ahead between houses and hotels, soon the beach and the **Bathing Pool** can be seen through the railings on the right.

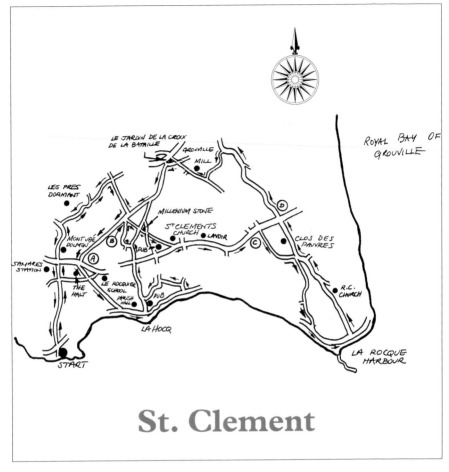

St. Clement

As 1 mile; 1.61 km. comes up on the cycle computer, we see a green traffic sign on our left. It reads " La Rocque Gorey A4 ", just after this sign we arrive at a mini roundabout. Turn right here, but remember that we have to give way to traffic coming from the right.

Cycle on, missing a road which enters from the left. After passing another road which comes in from the left, we see the rocky beach of **Grève D'Azette** over the sea wall to our right.

Cycle on past another left turning, situated directly opposite a slipway, and then past a car park which lies between this road and the beach.

Gradually the road begins to bend slightly to the left. As the bend begins to tighten look out for a sign ahead on a lamp-post, this will say **Green Island**. Being careful, turn right here. By now we will have cycled 2.7 miles; 4.35 km. Cycle on for a few more yards to reach our starting point in the car park.

The Route: Approximate distance 10.5 miles; 16.90 km.

Before we set off, look inland to your extreme left; in the copse of trees a few hundred yards away is hidden the Rocqueberg or Witches' Rock. This large rocky outcrop has a cloven hoofprint in its surface, and legend has it that it was a favourite meeting place for witches. Indeed of all the parishes, St.Clement has the most tales of witchcraft.

Leave the car park, and at the crossroads with the main coast road go straight over into **La Rue de Samares**. We find an unusual mix of both old and modern houses along this road, several appear to be 18th century. These homes are interspersed with cultivated fields, which endorses the relatively recent urbanisation of the parish.

Go through a crossroads, and as the lane rises we can see on the left one of the many stations of the Jersey Eastern Railway, Samares Station. When we draw level, it is possible to estimate the position of the line.

> The Jersey Eastern Railway ran from St.Helier to Gorey, between 1873 and 1929. A large proportion of the line ran through St.Clement, and we will see further signs of the railway as we make our way around the parish.

At the next crossroads go straight over and ascend into **La Blinerie**. Once under the shade of the tree, Samares Manor can be seen below on our left, whilst the Dolmen of Mont Ubé may be reached after a steep climb through the trees on our right.

The lane descends between pasture and we take the next right into a Green Lane. Our passage into Grouville is marked by the Green Lane signs on the left. The one that faces us announces our arrival into Grouville, whilst its counterpart does the same for St. Clement for people going in the opposite direction.

The wooded land to the left is **Les Pres Dormant**, an important area of wetland favoured by migrating birds during spring and autumn. After the lane bends sharply to the left, take a right turn up a hill following *Route 1*. Some way up the hill, take a right at a tiny crossroads, again following *Route 1*. The lane continues to climb and, after levelling out, we arrive at a T-junction.

Turn right here, and as we descend towards the sea again, a full panorama of St. Clement appears on our left. The large building in the foreground is **Le Rocquier School**, a secondary school which serves this part of the island. The lane steepens as we approach the yellow line. Here at the end of **Rue au Blancq (A)**, we have covered just over 2 miles; 3.22 km.

Cross over into a lane that comes in at an angle. After a hundred yards or so, we arrive at a crossroads. If we stop here, we should still be able to see the line of the railway on the left, with a row of derelict houses bordering the track. If we look over our shoulder towards a cream coloured cottage called **The Halt**, which was actually the crossing keeper's cottage, we should just be able to make out the line of the track heading back towards town. This seems quite remarkable as the railway has been closed for over 70 years.

Cycle on until the road borders a large field on the left. What appears to be a thick hedge of brambles at the rear of Le Rocquier School is in fact the embankment which carried the railway through the low lying fields.

At the end of this road, **Pontorson Lane**, turn left onto the coast road. We pass **St. Clement's Parish Hall** on our left, winner in 2001 of the best decorated parish hall during the annual flower festival. Staying on the coast road we pass between the public house and the Jersey round tower.

The road bends to the left and rises, then falls away again when the rocky beach of St.Clement's Bay appears on our right. At the bottom of the slope, turn left opposite the slipway into **Rue de Jambart**. Almost immediately after turn left into the Green Lane, **Rue du Prince**. Here we may see the more rural side of St.Clement, with green fields on the high ground to the right.

At the T-junction at the end of Rue du Prince turn left, after a yard or two stop and admire two aspects of St.Clement; on the right suburbia, the four tower blocks of Le Marais with a multitude of houses surrounding them. Then on the left, the full sweep of St.Clement's Bay with France on the horizon.

We climb a little further and soon this narrow lane winds back down to sea level. At the end of this lane, **Rue de la Hougette**, turn right. 100 yards or so up the lane is the headquarters of the Girls Brigade, look out for the owl perched on the roof.

When we reach the main road, leave **Rue du Hocq** and go straight over into **Rue de Pignon**. The road rises and some way up turn left into the Green Lane, **Rue de Genestet**. The hill is quite steep, so dismount and walk.

When we reach the yellow line at the end of Rue de Genestet, (**B**), we have cycled 4 miles; 6.44 km. Turn almost hairpin right into a very narrow Green Lane. We certainly will not meet any cars here, but do be aware that this lane crosses two minor roads on its way east, so be ready to brake. A fantastic view of nearly the whole parish can be seen as we freewheel along, the view being particularly good after passing the Millennium Stone, just before the lane begins to descend to the Parish church. To the left we see La Rocque harbour on the St. Clement's eastern border, whilst to the right the beach at Grève D'Azette marks the western end of the parish; out to sea Icho Tower guards the approaches to the bay.

When we reach the church, notice the huge tree standing in the graveyard, it is a yew tree which many believe to be the oldest tree in the island. Here turn left onto the main road. The building immediately after the church is the parish's first parish hall, built in 1878. I suspect it was not big enough, due to the rapid increase in population in the area during the twentieth century.

A little further on we come to a lavoir, built into the wall of a substantial farm. It was here that the women would gather to do their washing, and the seating built around the stream's exit allowed them to do so in some comfort.

Continue on a gentle freewheel and after a couple of slight bends turn right at a small crossroads into the Green Lane, **Rue des Nouettes (C)** which is on *Route 8* of the cycle network. At this point we have covered 5 miles; 8.05 km. St.Clement is a good locality for growing crops as the soil consists of loess, a fertile dust which was blown across from France during the cold dry spells the island endured many millions of years ago. At the next yellow line, turn right on *Route 8* into **Rue de la Louderie**.

Avoid a right turn and before long this lane meets the main coast road, **La Grande Route de Sablons**. We are now in Grouville for the next few miles, which can be seen by the red and white road signs unique to this parish.

Soon we arrive at **La Rocque Harbour**, a single granite jetty built in 1881.

> It was here on 6th January 1781, that the French landed under the command of Baron Phillipe de Rullecourt. De Rullecourt had initially chosen to land on the islet of L'Avarizon, a mile or more out to sea, where Seymour Tower now stands. But bad weather delayed his departure, and he was forced to land several days later at full tide at Plat Rocque, the headland where the present jetty starts. His invasion plans were thwarted by the brave 24 year old Major Francis Peirson who rallied his men, and defeated De Rullecourt in a 15 minute encounter in the Royal Square in St.Helier, later that day. Both Peirson and De Rullecourt were fatally wounded during the battle, and their bodies are buried at the Town Church.
>
> For bird watchers, La Rocque Harbour is a good place to watch several species of wading bird, depending on the season and the state of the tide.

We leave La Rocque and take the road on the left, opposite the slipway. Before arriving at **St.Peter La Rocque Catholic Church**, look out for a fireplace set into the wall at the entrance on the left. This is used as an imaginative site for the name of the house, **La Place de la Gare**, and though the building seems to have been built fairly recently, it certainly stands in the correct place for what would be La Rocque Station.

Follow this road as it twists and turns through the plain of St. Clement, after passing our exit of Rue des Nouettes, we come upon a granite wall on the left topped with dressed granite coping stones. Notice the inscription on the granite plaque **Don Gruchy -Clos des Pauvres - 1849**. The field behind the wall was given as a gift to the parish by a Miss Gruchy. The profits derived from renting it out being donated to the poor of the parish.

At the next crossroads, where we meet the main road again, cross directly over into **Rue des Côtils (D)**. We have now cycled just over 7 miles; 11.27 km. A fine view of the parish of Grouville opens up as we progress along this road, with Mont Orgueil castle dominating the horizon.

Once past the **Woodlands Apartments** on the left, the road allows us to freewheel down to an 'S' bend between two high granite walls. After passing a green hand pump, set in a charming granite alcove, turn immediately hairpin left into a steep lane with which we will regain the heights before our descent back to Green Island. As usual I would recommend walking as it is quite steep. Our efforts are rewarded with a good view of the castle, seen over our shoulder as we climb.

When we reach level ground, **Grouville Mill** is seen ahead. The mill tower is now the central part of a modern dwelling, though during the war the occupying forces used the mill as an observation post. The very top of the tower was added by the Germans to give them a full 360-degree perspective over the eastern side of the island.

On reaching the T-junction turn right towards the mill. Miss a lane coming in from the left, and continue on until we reach a crossroads opposite a triangular copse of trees. This small patch of land is called **Le Jardin de la Croix de la Bataille**. It was here in 1406 that Pero Nino a Castilian pirate, and Hector de Pontbriand a Breton knight engaged a force dispatched from Mont Orgeuil castle. With such ferocity was the battle fought, that the hill disappearing to the right of the junction flowed with blood, and to this day it is commonly known as Blood Hill.

Turn left here and left again shortly after into **Rue au Blancq**. We can enjoy our last panoramic view of St.Clement along this stretch of road. After missing a lane entering from the left, take the next right retracing our steps on *Route 1*.

This lane descends, and as it does it gives us a glimpse of the eastern side of St. Helier on the left. Turn left at the tiny crossroads and follow the lane to the T-junction at the bottom. Here turn left on *Route 1*, following the road as it bends to the right. At the next T-junction abandon *Route 1* and turn left into the Green Lane, the lane rising as we pass the Mont Ubé Dolmen once more.

This lane falls away quickly as we approach the yellow line, so be ready to brake. Using care, exit **La Blinierie** and cross over into **Rue de Samares**.

Follow Rue de Samares back to our starting point at **Green Island**. At the final junction, I would suggest walking along the pavement on the left and crossing where the road is straighter.

St. Peter
The Green Lane Parish

St. Peter offers us a rich mix of the past and the present, all enveloped in very rural surroundings. Though the parish is in the west of the island, it is nevertheless quite high and we find ourselves looking out over some far reaching views.

Getting there: Approximate distance 2.6 miles; 4.18 km.

Leave **Liberation Square**, using the crossing to make your way across the dual carriageway, going towards the harbour. Once on the quayside, turn right and head west towards the underpass. Cycle parallel to the road as the pavement rises, and using care cross the two roads that lead to the Elizabeth Terminal.

On the far side the cycle track is a rough gravel path which runs for about 100 yards, before being bisected by the car park sliproad. Soon the gravel becomes granite paving as we ride alongside the old sea wall. Here the cycle track is marked by a single white line running parallel to the sea wall. As we leave the sea wall, the cycleway is defined by two white lines. By 0.55 miles; 0.89 km. we will pass the **Grand Hotel** on the right, at West Park.

The track follows the sea wall to St.Aubin, the small village at the far end of the bay. In doing so, it mimics the Jersey Railway Company's line to St.Aubin, which ran at the turn of the 20th century. In fact the sea wall was built to protect the line from the ravages of the sea.

As a guide to mileage, we will pass the café opposite the Jersey Round Tower, at **First Tower** in 1.31 miles; 2.11 km. The

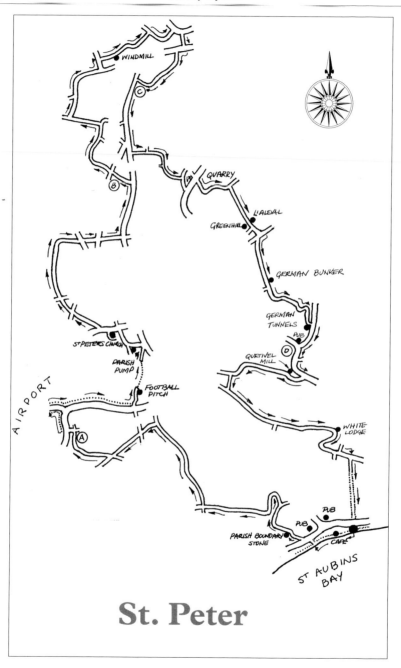

St. Peter

burger bar at the end of Victoria Avenue in 2.12 miles; 3.41 km. and, our destination, the small car park with the white railings, in 2.57 miles; 4.14 km.

The car park is easy to find; it is sandwiched between the road and the cycle track. There is a phone box at the far end, and it has a cycle *Route 4* sign at one corner.

The Route: Approximate distance 11.5 miles; 18.51 km.

Our starting point is the small car park that lies between the corner of Bel Royal and the Beaumont roundabout, on the seaward side of the road.

Using the cycle track that runs between the car park and the seawall, turn right and head west towards the small harbour at St. Aubin. Cycle over a slipway and between a Jersey Round Tower and a café. At the next slipway turn inland to join the main road. Using care, turn left onto the main road and then right very soon after into **Ruelle es Ruaux**. After a slight S-bend we re-enter St. Peter. Notice the small boundary stone on the left and the telltale line in the tarmac where one parish meets another.

Follow the lane as it bends right and, then bear left up the rough surface of **Mont des Vignes**. After the hairpin bend, take the opportunity to look to your left and enjoy a small section of St. Aubin's Bay in the distance. Once we have reached the summit a further view of the island can be seen over our right shoulder. Cycle on and at the crossroads turn right into **Rue des Vignes**.

A good stretch of level road lies ahead. In relation to the rest of the island we are quite high up here and, if we look to the right, most of the island can be seen. In fact it is even possible to make out the IBA transmitter mast at Frémont on the north coast.

At the next junction turn left into **Rue Cappelain**. Continue over the next crossroads into **Rue des Sauvalleries**. As we go further the tall hedgerows make the lanes seem like a maze. In the midst of this maze we find another crossroads, where we turn right into **Rue de Saut Falluet**. A swift descent takes us through a right and left swoop into a small valley. Just as suddenly the lane rises again and, after a right turn, we emerge at a tiny crossroads. Here at the end of Rue de Saut Falluet, (**A**) we have cycled 2.6 miles; 4.18 km.

Turn left and, after dismounting, turn right onto the pavement so that we can cross over to the gravel cycle track on the far side of the road. Using great care, cross this busy road and join the cycle track.

Follow the track, carefully crossing the airport road, to continue on the other side. Where it ends, turn left onto a heavily patched stretch of tarmac. The road ends opposite St. Peter's Parish football pitch and we are required to walk a short distance until we meet tarmac again on the other side of the airfield.

> We get an excellent view of the runway here. It is hard to imagine how much the airport has grown since it was built in 1937. Before then the airborne traveller would have landed on the beach at West Park, the arrival and departure time being governed by the tide. In 1937, the main airport building was put up and aircraft landed on grass runways. During the Occupation the Germans increased the size of the airfield and laid tarmac runways. They used granite from Ronez Quarry for the foundations, which was transported through St. Mary on a small railway.

When we meet tarmac again, remount and cycle a few yards to the yellow line where we turn left into **Rue de St. Clement**. Pass the parish pump on the left and bear right into **Rue des Fosses**. This pump appears to be a remnant of its former glory; a very utilitarian structure stands behind it. I like the sign that says that only parishioners can use it. Fortunately there are a couple of pubs nearby that will serve anyone!

Pass the community centre and the beautiful granite parish

hall on the left and, after dismounting, walk the short distance to the main road. At the main road remount and cycle past **St. Peter's Parish Church**.

St. Peter's Church is quite big by local standards. It was enlarged in 1886 to accommodate the troops that were living in barracks on what is now the south end of the airfield and who used it as their local church.

Once we reach the primary school on the left, turn right into **Rue du Bocage**.

Rue du Bocage is an interesting mix of old and new houses. The village developments that we see around the island are something fairly new. Previously no house could be built in the countryside unless surrounded by 20 vergées of arable land. A vergée is a local unit of area, two and a quarter vergées being equivalent to an acre. At the time, it was felt that the island was rapidly becoming overrun with apple orchards and there would be no land given over to the production of grain.

Leaving Rue du Bocage, cross over into **Rue des Niemes**. Continue along Rue des Niemes, crossing over a crossroads as we do so. The lane falls away slightly as we leave the village. The tall wall on the right appears to be built in layers. The reason for this is that the masons of the time were paid by the length of wall built, the height being constant. The lane skirts the wall and bends to the right. It climbs gently and we arrive at a junction with the main road. Using great care cross over this busy road into **La Neuve Route**.

Travel along this short stretch of road until we reach a deliberately staggered crossroads. Here, cross straight over into **Les Routeurs** and freewheel down the hill. On reaching another crossroads turn left into **Route des Hetres**. We pass a long granite wall, punctuated only by a granite arched doorway. Again we are quite high up here. A glance to our right reveals the rock face of the quarry at Gigoulande in St. Peter's Valley and the spire of St. Matthew's Church in St. Lawrence.

Cycle a little further and take the first left into **Rue D'Auvergne**. At the yellow line at the end of Rue D'Auvergne (**B**) we have covered 4.98 miles; 8.02km. Before crossing, notice the impressive water pump on the right. It was only at the end of the 19th century that water was piped into homes, and that was initially only in the town area.

Being careful, cross the junction into **Rue D'Elysee**. Follow the lane as it bends to the right, and passes across a narrow run of cobbles. Miss a turning on the right and take the next left, still in Rue D'Elysee. After passing a low wall on the right, turn right into **Rue de la Forge**. Continue into **La Preterie**, avoiding a lane that enters from the left. The lane bends right and we pass a row of cottages. At the yellow line turn left into **Chemin de L'Eglise** and, very soon after, turn right into a narrow lane.

This lane is actually in St. Ouen but the fields to the right are in St. Peter, as is the windmill which we will pass shortly. The mill was built in 1837, the money for its construction being raised by public subscription. These days the mill is a public house and restaurant, and its sails are merely for decoration.

Cycle on until we arrive at a T-junction, where we turn right. We pass another village development on our right as we approach the yellow line at the end of **Rue Mahier**. At this junction go straight ahead and immediately right into a 30mph zone. We can freewheel for a moment until the next yellow line where we turn right and then left soon after. This charming detour allows us to avoid the traffic on the busy main road. When the lane does emerge onto the main road, at the end of **Rue es Viberts**, **(C)** we have cycled 7.0 miles; 11.27km. Turn left onto the main road.

Cycle along the main road for roughly a quarter of a mile, missing a turning on the right. The road forks and we need to bear left, taking the first left immediately after into **Rue des Sillions**. This lane takes us down into St. Peter's Valley. After passing a left turn, it descends gently between an avenue of gnarled trees. The lane bends to the right and a much clearer view of the quarry can be seen on the left. Miss a lane that comes in from the right and begin the very steep descent of **Les Charrieres**. This hill is exceptionally steep and in places very slippery, so it may be wise to walk down.

At the bottom of the hill, turn right and then left on reaching the main valley road. The road climbs gently and we need to take the first right into **Mont Remon**. We need our lowest gear for this hill or alternatively walking is always an attractive option.

As we draw near to the summit, a gap in the bank on the left allows us a view of the quarry workings below. This is one of three quarries currently being worked on the island. In days gone by, it was normal to quarry stone as close to the building site as possible, which explains the many small excavations we see around.

At the top of Mont Remon, where a profusion of choices is available, turn right into **Rue de L'Aleval**.

This road affords us a splendid view of St. Peter's Valley and the land on the far side of the valley. From this view point we can see St. Peter's Church, La Hague Manor with its square tower and, if we look behind us, we might just spy the top of the windmill through the trees. We pass between two magnificent examples of 17th century Jersey architecture as we head towards the yellow line. On our left we see L'Aleval and it is matched on the opposite side of the road by Greenhill.

Miss the right turn immediately after **Greenhill**, and bear left up to the yellow line. Here turn right and then left into **Rue de Coin Varin**.

This road is a continuation of the ridge we were riding along a moment ago. Across to our right we can see the landing lights of the airport, but on our left is something more unusual. Almost in the middle of the field is a German bunker, carefully disguised as a house complete with chimney pots.It is quite unusual to find bunkers so obviously above ground, but this is one of at least three in the area.

Pass a right turn and continue until a bend in the road. Here we are able to see the sea between the valley walls and we can just see the right-hand side of Elizabeth Castle in St. Aubin's Bay. Freewheel on. The lane twists and turns and makes its way along a wooded slope, running parallel to a wide smooth road below. This is **Route de L'Aleval**, known locally as the German Road, although it was only officially opened in 1966. When we emerge on this road, turn right and follow the slope down, looking out for the entrance to some German tunnels just after the cottages on the right. Nowadays the tunnels are used for growing mushrooms. Freewheel down to the yellow line (**D**) opposite the public house. By this point we have come 9.40 miles.

Turn left and carry on along the valley road, **La Vallée de St. Pierre**. Pass a turning on the left and, after the road has swung left, using care turn right into **Mont Fallu**.

At the foot of the hill stands **Quetivel Mill**, which dates from the early 14th Century. Like several other mills, it was pressed into use during the German Occupation, but fell into disuse soon after. In 1969 it was badly damaged by fire, but was restored in the late 1970s. During the summer months the mill is open for the sale of flour and other goods.

Ascend this, the last hill on our ride today. Though not steep, it is quite long, so feel free to walk. After the S bend at the top, take the lane on the left into **Rue Verte**, aptly enough a Green Lane. At the end of Rue Verte turn left into **La Rue de la Fontaine**. We can almost freewheel back to the start from here.

After passing a road on the right, La Rue de la Fontaine becomes **Les Grupieaux**, and the hill begins to steepen. We round a right-hand bend and see on the left **White Lodge**,

White Lodge, a house built in 1934 in the fashionable International Style. The house was designed by Arthur Grayson, an architect whose distinctive work can also be seen at Les Lumieres in St.Brelade and The Glass Church at Millbrook. Descend a little further and the whole of St.Aubin's Bay appears before us.

Follow the hill down and, after passing a road on the right and a turning off to the left, take the narrow tarmac lane on the right. This lane follows *Route 4* of the cycle network. Continue ahead as the tarmac turns to a gravel track that accompanies a stream on the right. On reaching the road, use the crossing to regain our starting point.

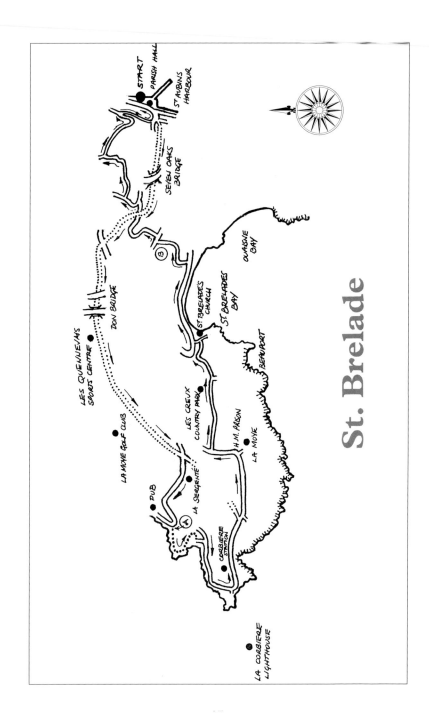

St. Brelade

St. Brelade

On track to the lighthouse

St. Brelade has the longest coastline of all the parishes, but not alas the greatest number of quiet lanes. However, it does have the gravel track of the old Jersey Railway Company, which runs neatly through the middle of the parish and we will use this for some of our route.

Getting there*: Approximate distance 3.5 miles; 5.63 km.*

Leave **Liberation Square** and using the crossing, cross the dual carriageway, going towards the harbour. On reaching the quayside turn right and head west. Ride parallel to the road, and after a slight rise cross the two roads which lead to the Elizabeth Terminal.

Ride over a short stretch of gravel until we reach granite paving stones and a stout granite wall on the left. A white line and a bicycle logo on the stone heralds the beginning of the cycle track which takes us straight to our starting point.

We will follow this track for the next few miles completely away from any motor traffic, but do not forget that the promenade is shared with walkers, roller bladers and other cyclists, so proceed with caution.

After about 0.55 miles; 0.89 km. we pass the **Grand Hotel**, from this point the track is marked by two parallel white lines. By the **Old Station Café**, which is across the road from the car showrooms, we will have cycled 1.75 miles; 2.82 km. Continue on past the *Route 4* turn-off beside the white railings and we reach **Collette's Cabin** at the bottom of **La Haule Hill** in 3.20 miles; 5.15 km.

We make our way towards the large white building ahead, staying on the pavement until we draw level with the petrol station. As soon as we pass the petrol station, turn left into the car park. By now we have cycled 3.5 miles; 5.63 km.

The Route: Approximate distance 9.25 miles; 14.89 km.

We leave the car park and head between **St. Brelade's Parish Hall**, the large white building, and the sea wall. When the small harbour of St. Aubin appears before us, bear right passing the front of the parish hall, and head up the hill. Pass the bank and, where a hill comes in from the left, bear left onto a stretch of tarmac which has KEEP CLEAR painted on it. This is also sign posted *Route 1* The Railway Track.

The orange gravel of the track soon comes into view, but look out for the tunnel on the left, which was quarried out of the rock in 1898 to give the line a straighter run out of St. Aubin. Further tunnels were dug by the Germans during the last war, using this tunnel as a starting point. Nowadays the tunnels are used for storage, though one tunnel is used by the St. Brelade's Smallbore Rifle Club as a rifle range.

The line curves and climbs very slightly. Between here and Don Bridge, a mile and a half away, the gradient is a mere 1 in 40, Surprisingly, this was considered quite steep by the engineers who built the line.

The Railway Track is bound on each side by dense vegetation for much of its length, and this together with a complete absence of cars, makes it a very appealing route. The gentle gradient also allows us to gain height at an easy pace.

The route to Corbière is crossed by two bridges, and the first at Seven Oaks comes into view before long. Built in 1875, this bridge carries the road which runs from St. Aubin to St. Brelade. The track is also bisected by a number of roads as it heads west. We come across the first of these after a mile or so. Using great care, cross over and continue on. A blue cycle route sign: *Route 1* Les Quennevais and Corbière appears ahead.

We cycle through **Pont Marquet Country Park**, and soon we have to cross another road. Again being careful, cross over. The low bridge we see ahead is Don Bridge. So named as this area is called Don Farm, after an experimental farm set up here in the early 1800s by the then Lieutenant-Governor of the island General Sir George Don.

We are now beginning to get into a fairly built-up area, quite a different scene to that which the passengers would have enjoyed in the train's heyday. Until the 1960s, most of this area was sand dunes, and Don Farm station would have been busiest when the Bank Holiday race-goers would have taken the train out to the horse racing at Les Quennevais. The race course would have been situated roughly opposite what is now **Les Quennevais Sports Centre**, which is a few yards further on. The sports ground is enclosed by a purpose built cycle track which is used for cycle racing during the summer months. This stretch of the route is bordered on the left by housing, broken only by a modern secondary school.

Soon we reach open country again, albeit in the form of **La Moye Golf Club**. On the left is the driving range, while on the right is the course. We get our first glimpse of the sea just beyond the clubhouse. Cross over two tarmac lanes. Once on gravel again we find the gradient in our favour. Freewheel down to the main road and using care turn right. Before the hill begins to descend, look to your left. The cement-rendered dwelling called **La Sergenté**, was the home of Jean Martel, founder of the world famous cognac house.

As we start to freewheel down the hill, look out for the water trough built into the bank on the right. I suspect it would have given a welcome drink to horses pulling cart loads of vraic up the hill. Vraic is the local name for seaweed. It has been used for centuries as a natural fertiliser, being rich in potash and trace elements. But with the advent of tractors it lost favour, as tractors rust a lot faster than horses do !. I'm happy to report that it is regaining some of its popularity, it is often said that the vraic gives our new potatoes their unique flavour.

The road descends and a fantastic view of St. Ouen's Bay unfolds before us. Where the road bends sharply right, bear left, and return onto a gravel path, following *Route 1* to Corbière. By now we have cycled 3.4 miles; 5.47 km. (**A**).

Here we are able to get a panoramic view of the whole bay; with **La Rocco Tower** in the middle distance and the headland of L'Etacq at the far corner. This track takes us around the headland and into the rocky bay of **Petit Port**. We pass close to two or three bunkers, remnants of the last war. The island was heavily fortified during the German Occupation, and it is claimed that a fifth of all the concrete in Hitler's Atlantic Wall can be found in Jersey.

On arriving at the end of the gravel track turn left, and then turn right when we meet the main road. We are able to freewheel for a short while but be warned that beyond the bend is a steep climb, so change down a gear or two in anticipation. As usual, I would recommend walking if you find it hard going. To the right, **Corbière lighthouse** and its rocky environs can be seen as we climb.

On reaching the corner, I suggest we take a breather and enjoy one of the most picturesque views the island can offer. Corbière lighthouse was built in 1873, and has the distinction of being the first concrete lighthouse built in the British Isles. As we can see from the memorial beside the road to the lighthouse, seafaring disasters are not necessarily a thing of the past. The sculpture records the St. Malo Disaster, when on April 17th 1995, a passenger ferry en route from Jersey to Sark and Guernsey ran aground on the rocks in the foreground, fortunately without loss of life.

Corbière Lighthouse (left); St. Malo Memorial (right)

We leave La Corbière and climb the last few yards of the hill.

> The tower on the right is a German sighting tower, once used for directing artillery fire but now home to Jersey Radio. Jersey Radio controls the maritime movements around the island. At the summit, on the left stands a fine dressed granite building, this was Corbière station, the end of the line.

A pleasant section of level tarmac takes us parallel to the railway track seen on our left, whilst the two walls we see on the right are the remains of the wheelhouse of **La Rosière Quarry**. A spur line, which ran to the quarry, can be seen coming in from the left. Follow the road as it bends left, passing H.M.Prison La Moye on the right, just beyond the trees. Then take the next right into **La Rue des Champs** going toward Beauport.

After passing a number of houses, the countryside opens up again and we pass the parkland of **Les Creux Country Park** on the left and the beach at **Beauport** on the right. Looking straight ahead we see the cliffs at Ouaisné, which is at the far end of the bay into which we are now descending. Be ready on your brakes as the steep hill worms itself down to **St. Brelade's Church**.

The church is well worth a visit, especially the small chapel on the right, as it has 14th century wall paintings inside. Unlike other churches, these pictures have survived the Reformation because at the time the chapel was used to house the two artillery pieces each parish possessed.

Upon leaving the churchyard, look at the inscription inside the lych gate. Jesse Boot, founder of Boots the chemist, married a Jersey girl, Florence Rowe. They retired here and were great benefactors to the island. Jesse Boot is buried just around the headland, and his grave can be found by following the lane which leads to the left between the church and the far graveyard. An unmarked tarmac path on the right-hand side of the lane is the only clue to the whereabouts of the grave.

Leaving the church turn right and follow a slight slope down to the yellow line. Turn right here and proceed along this road. St. Brelade's Bay is described as Jersey's premier holiday beach. This is quite understandable when we see its flat sands and inviting waters. Continue along the road and, just after a 30mph sign at the foot of the hill, turn left into a Green Lane. This is quite a taxing climb, so I'd suggest walking. When we reach the yellow line at the top of **Mont Gras D'Eau** we will have come 7.3 miles; 11.75 km. (**B**).

Turn right here and cycle along the main road for a few yards until we take the first left into the Green Lane, **Mont Nicolle**. A very welcome freewheel follows, and eventually the lane levels out in a valley. We pass under the railway bridge that we crossed on our way out to Corbière. The lane rises gradually and at the yellow line turn left, again we keep ascending at a comfortable pace. Notice the granite post that makes the corner, it has directions to the outlying parishes inscribed on it. Ascend this gentle hill as it curves to the right and in due course take the first right into **Rue du Bocage**.

We are now on the heights above St. Aubin and to our right we can see the valley in which the railway track runs. The lane meanders along, twisting left, right and left again. Before long it meets a road coming in from the right, **Mont de la Rocque**. Turn right into this road and begin a long freewheel that will take us back into the heart of St. Aubin. The road bends slightly to the right and suddenly St. Aubin appears in front of us. Go a little further down and, at the yellow line, turn hairpin right into **Rue du Croquet** or **St. Aubin's High Street**. Once again a fine view over the bay and the fort presents itself.

We are now in the old commercial heart of Jersey, the buildings on either side of the street align themselves with prosperous times in the island's history; cod fishing, privateering and boat building.

At the end of the High Street turn left and follow the road back to our starting point.

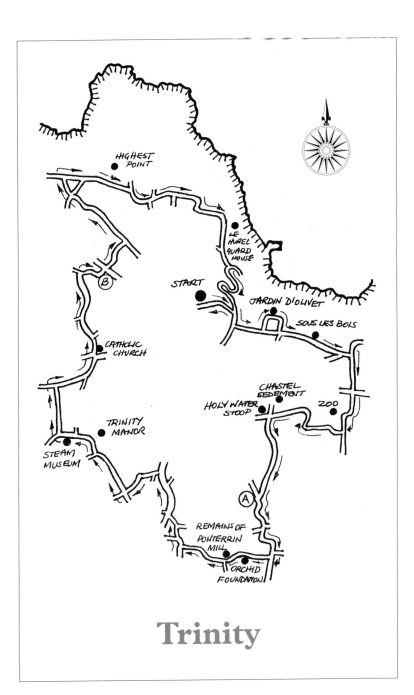

Trinity

Trinity

A high speed parish

Today we visit Trinity, literally the high spot of our rides around Jersey. Although all the northern parishes are further from sea level than their counterparts in the south, Trinity can claim the highest point on the island at 455 feet.

Getting there: Approximate distance 5.72 miles; 9.21 km.

Leave **Liberation Square** and head north up **Conway Street**, which is just to the left of the **Pomme D'Or Hotel**. When the road forks, rather than going left into **Broad Street**, or right into **Library Place**, dismount and walk straight ahead into **New Street**. Cross the pedestrian precinct and remount in New Street, where there are fewer pedestrians.

Cycle on up to the yellow line and turn left into **Union Street**. Pass through a crossroads and take the next right, using care as we cross the flow of traffic. Bear right, miss a left and then a right turn, and turn left after the pedestrian crossing into **Great Union Road**. Continue up Great Union Road, passing a left and then taking the second turning right into **Dorset Street**. Carry on through a crossroads and, where the street bends to the left, dismount and cross a short stretch of pavement into the continuation of this street. Remount and follow the street round to arrive at a yellow line. Here turn left and cycle up to the traffic lights at the crossroads of **David Place** and **Val Plaisant**.

When the lights change, go straight over, miss a left and a right, and continue up to the next set of lights. At these lights, proceed ahead into the right-hand lane. Here, go straight on into **Trinity Road**, After 200 yards, we reach a fork in the road, bear right using care into **Les Vaux New Road** on *Route 7*. Pass a turning on the right and then two on the left. Miss another road on the right, before passing the tennis courts. The road rises and bends to the left, passing a hill on the right. The road swings right and we pass through another S-bend, missing a road from the left this time.

Continue along the valley road, avoiding a Green Lane on the left, until we reach a fork in the road. Here we have come 1.96 miles; 3.15km. Take the right fork and cycle on past the reservoir. The road rises and descends as we approach a left-hand bend in the road. Follow the road around to the left, again following *Route 7*, and avoiding a hill on the right. After passing a lane on the right, we arrive at the foot of **Mont de la Rosière**. This is very steep so walk up and save your energy for later.

When the road levels out, pass a turning on the right and then one, a little further on, on the left. Miss another left at the end of the road, just before *Route 7* ends in **La Rue de la Boucterie** in **Victoria Village**. At the end of *Route 7*, turn right and follow *Route 3* up a narrow lane. Pass a left, the lane meanders left and right, and arrives at a junction with a cycle route sign post. By now we have cycled 3.50 miles; 5.63 km. Here turn left into **Rue de Dielament**, following *Route 3A*.

Miss a left and freewheel along, passing a war memorial before the lane bends left. Follow the lane as it makes its way between fields and hedgerows. We pass a lane on the right, then another on the left. A shallow slope takes us to a crossroads, where we leave **Rue de la Piece Mauger** and cross over into **Rue de Pot de Rocher**. At this point we will have come 4.59 miles; 7.39km.

Take the first left into **Rue du Becquet** and, where the road forks, bear right into **Rue des Bouillons**. The road climbs slightly and we go through a crossroads into **Chemin D'Olivet**. At the T-junction, at the end of Chemin D'Olivet, turn right and follow *Route 1*. Where this road meets the hill, at the yellow line, turn left and climb for 200 yards before turning right into the gravel car park at **Le Parc de la Petite Falaise**. This is our starting point for our Trinity ride.

The Route: Approximate distance 9 Miles; 14.48 km.

Our route starts at the car park situated at the top of Bouley Bay, next to the common or what is now called **Le Parc de la Petite Falaise**. The car park is built on the site of the old Bouley Bay Hotel, which was knocked down in the early seventies.

Leaving the car park we turn left and freewheel down **La Rue de la Petite Falaise**. Where the road joins the main hill, using care, turn right into **La Route du Boulay**.

When the road levels out we take a left into **Chemin D'Olivet**. After 200 yards detour into the lane on the left to pass **Jardin d'Olivet**, an area of common land, where in 1549 the local militia successfully defended the island from a French invasion force which had just ransacked Sark. At the far end of the common stands the most impressive 'No Dumping' sign in the island.

Follow the road round, and at the crossroads, leave **Rue de la Falaise** and turn left into **Rue des Bouillons**. Enjoy the slight slope that takes us past a relatively unchanged 17th century cottage; **Sous les Bois**.

Continue over the yellow line at the end of Rue des Bouillons. At the T-junction, leave **Rue du Becquet** and turn right into **Rue du Pot du Rocher**. Another gentle freewheel takes us to the main road, which we cross to enter **Rue de la Piece Mauger**.

For the next half mile we will be skirting the grounds of Les Augres Manor or **Jersey Zoo** as it is better known. The road winds right and left. The large building that we see on the right is the Lowland Gorilla enclosure. Lowland Gorillas were one of the

Above: Holy water stoop at Les Cateaux

Above: 'No Dumping' sign at Jardin d'Olivet

'Sous Les Bois'

first endangered species cared for by the Jersey Wildlife Preservation Trust.

Take the first right into a narrow lane. This lane provides us with a good view of the Orang-Utan enclosure and also the manor house itself, just visible through the trees.

The lane descends between two high leafy banks. When it rises again, look to the right across the field. The tall mound which makes the far corner is all that remains of a huge earthwork known as **Chastel Sedement**. It was said to extend to 10 acres, and be enclosed by a moat. Islanders would flee into it during raids, taking with them their family and as much livestock as they could round up.

Before turning left at the crossroads at the end of **Rue de la Fosse**, notice the granite bowl built into the wall opposite, above the mounting block. This appears to be a holy water stoop, probably taken from a church demolished during the Reformation.

As the lane drops away into a wooded valley, the white buildings which we see in the distance are what is left of Dielament Manor, once the largest fief in the island. At the end of **Rue des Cateaux (A)**, we have cycled 2.62 miles; 4.22 km. Bear left and follow the lane as it twists its way up to Victoria Village. As we climb, avoid a lane on the left and then another on the right.

Follow the hill as it bends left and right as it climbs. At the top, when we reach **Rue de la Boucterie**, miss a left and turn right into **Rue du Moulin de Ponterrin**. Once past the Eric Young Orchid Foundation, the lane gets quite steep, so be ready with your brakes. Just before the bottom of the hill we pass the remains of **Ponterrin Mill**. At the yellow line, cross over and ascend the only steep hill on our ride today.

Thankfully, the road soon levels out. At the T-junction at the top of **Rue du Moulin de Ponterrin** turn right. Follow the road round and turn right into **Rue du Clos Durell**. Proceed along this road, missing a right, until it meets the main road after a slight rise.

Ruins of Ponterrin Mill

At the main road turn right and, after a short distance, turn left into **Rue Jacques**. Pass a lane on the left and, on reaching the crossroads, turn right. Continue along this typical Jersey lane past a lane on the left. Soon **Trinity Manor** can be seen through the trees on the right. The manor owes its chateau-like appearance to Mr. Athelstan Riley, who restored the manor in the early part of the 20th century.

Once past the radio masts on the corner, miss a right and carry on down **La Rue Bechet**, passing the **Young Farmers' Club** and the **Steam Museum**, before turning right into **La Neuve Route**. At the end of the road take a right and head back toward the church steeple. Coast along this stretch, avoiding a lane that enters from the right and, when the road divides at the Catholic Church, avoid the appealingly named Rue de la Monnaie and bear left into **Rue de la Fontaine**.

Go past a lane on the left and then another on the right. The road climbs and, after passing a dead end sign on the left, becomes **La Rue Countanche**. The road winds to the right. On the skyline we can see Ebenezer Methodist Church and the Highfield Hotel. Continue up this road and take the first right into **Rue de la Fontaine de Colarde**. The lane dips and, after turning left, climbs again to meet the main road.

By now we have come 6.2 miles; 9.98 km. (**B**). Exercising some care, turn right and, after only a few yards, turn left into **L'Allee**. At the T-junction turn left and begin a long freewheel which takes us to a small crossroads. Here leave **La Rue du Nord** and go straight over the junction into **Rue de la Petite Lande**.

> On reaching the yellow line we get our first glimpse of the sea, with Sark away in the distance. Nowadays an aeronautical receiving station graces the high ground on the right, but twenty years ago a disused coach was the only feature of the area. In it lived an old lady and her entourage of dogs. Rumour had it that if the dogs did not keep you away, the shotgun she often brandished would!

Turn right here and, missing a right, follow the road past the twin masts of the transmitter station. Behind the building is Jersey's highest point at 455 feet. The road dips and passes through an S-bend, missing a lane on the left, before rising again. It passes another lane on the right and, at the next corner continue straight on into **La Vieille Charrière**.

The lane curves and falls away as we make the long descent towards the harbour at Bouley Bay. When the lane straightens out, we can see a ruined Napoleonic guardhouse on the hillside in front of us. This is one of a chain which would relay signals from Gorey to Grosnez and from there on to Guernsey.

Freewheel down this long descent, passing a lane on the right some way down. At the yellow line, we leave La Vieille Charrière at Les Platons corner and start our ascent of the nationally famous Bouley Bay hillclimb course. Although the hill is generally associated with motor sport, there are also opportunities for the more masochistic, as cycling and running races are held here as well. Continue up the hill, avoiding a detour to the left at Radio Corner, the tightest hairpin on the hill.

After rounding the final hairpin take time to admire the double armco barrier which protects a small patch of level ground, on which stand two benches and a refuse bin.

> This is where club officials sit when a hillclimb is in progress. Until the mid-seventies, it was felt that a single armco barrier would provide sufficient protection against any errant competitor. However, after an incident in which an 'E' type Jaguar nearly decimated the clubs hierarchy at a stroke, the height of the barrier was doubled to its present height!

After enjoying the outlook from this vantage point, climb the remainder of the hill, following the road as it swings right into **La Rue de la Petite Falaise** again. Climb a little further to get back to the start.

Grouville

Water Wonderland

Grouville has one of the largest areas of wetland in Jersey and is therefore, in prospect, a very flat and marshy parish. This is not entirely the case: our trip around the parish will reveal some inspiring views and tranquil valleys.

Getting there: Approximate distance 5.75 miles; 9.25 km.

Leave **Liberation Square** and head north up **Conway Street**, which is just to the left of the **Pomme D'Or Hotel**. After 150 yards or so turn right into **Bond Street**. At the crossroads go straight over into **Pier Road** and ascend the hill. Once past the multi-storey car park on the left bear left and climb a little further. Follow the road as it bends to the left and descends slightly beneath some trees. By the time we reach the next junction we will have come 0.7 miles; 1.13km. Turn left and descend the hill, continuing straight on ahead past hotels and in due course the **Bathing Pool**.

After passing the Bathing Pool we arrive at a roundabout. Here we have to give way to traffic coming from the right, so, when the road is clear, turn right. Follow this road for a short distance and then bear left into **Green Road**. At the traffic lights we have cycled 1.60 miles; 2.58 km. Turn left and cycle on to the bend ahead. Where the road bends to the left, using care, turn right into **La Blinerie**, a Green Lane. Follow this pleasant lane past the golf course and take the first left. As soon as the lane has turned sharp left, turn right at the foot of a hill, following *Route 1*. Climb the hill and turn right at the tiny crossroads halfway up. Climb a

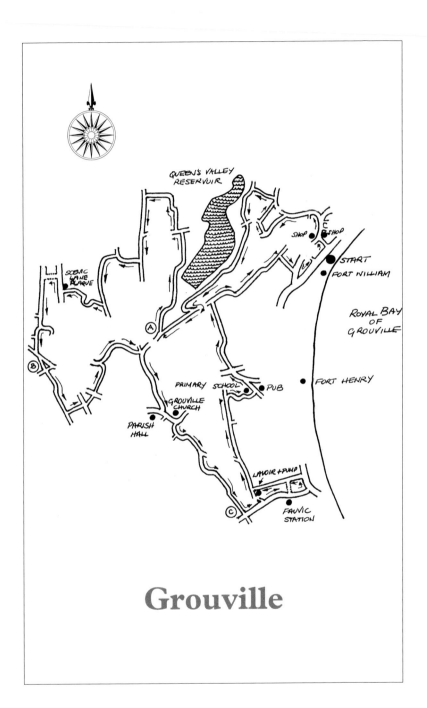

Grouville

little further until we reach a yellow line where we turn left. Continue on to the yellow line at the end of this road. Here we meet the main road at the top of **Grouville Hill**. By now we have cycled 3.56 miles; 5.73 km.

We need to turn right here and freewheel down the hill, missing a left turn. Just after passing a small car park on the left, turn hairpin left into **La Rue de Grouville**. Cycle past three lanes that emerge from the left and, after the road bends right and begins to climb, bear right following *Route 1*. At the next fork, bear right again, still on *Route 1*. The lane climbs and we carry on past a hill that comes in from the left and then a lane which ascends from the right.

Proceed along this smooth lane, taking the first right, which brings us into **Gorey Village**. At the T-junction, turn right and then left at the junction with the main road. After a short distance, turn right into the large gravel car park.

The Route: Approximate distance 10 miles; 16.09 km.

Our ride starts in the gravel car park opposite the village green in **Gorey Village**. Leave the car park and turn right along the main road for a short distance, before turning left to make our way into the heart of the village. Where the road divides, take a right turn and continue on between the houses and the shops, missing two narrow lanes that come in from the right. At the far end of the village, where the road forks, take the left fork and begin an ascent of the hill that overlooks the village.

The hill steepens as we climb, so I would suggest dismounting at the junction with the NO ENTRY sign. Bear left at this fork and walk the rest of the way, stopping at the second field entrance on the left.

Here we get a fantastic panoramic view of the castle, Gorey Village and the Royal Bay of Grouville. We can see that the village has grown recently, but the most dramatic growth was in the 1820s when English oyster fishermen, together with their wives and families established themselves in the village. These people were from Kent, where over-fishing had left the oyster beds near Whitstable empty. The oyster beds off Gorey eventually met with the same fate. Hardly a surprise when we consider that each of the 200 boats in the fishing fleet were taking around 12,000 oysters a day!

Gorey was the birthplace of one of golf's greatest heroes; Harry Vardon, 6 time winner of the British Open and originator of the "Vardon Grip". Harry was brought up in a cottage on the edge of the course and as a boy he played with homemade clubs and marbles.

Notice the small house on the edge of the golf course, overlooking the beach. A closer look will reveal that it is built on a Napoleonic fort; **Fort William**. It is surrounded by a dry moat, now the garden, and even has a drawbridge. Fort William was one of eight defences that protected this vulnerable coastline.

After enjoying the view, walk to the summit and bear right at the fork. Pass a Green Lane on the left and continue onto the yellow line. Here we turn left and then immediately left again into a narrow, little used Green Lane. Freewheel down the slope and turn left at the bottom. We get our first glimpse of **Queen's Valley Reservoir** on the right, with St. Saviour's Hospital above it. We will trace the edge of the reservoir for the next mile or two.

Follow the lane as it bends and climbs, only to descend briefly to a tiny crossroads which we go through. Climb again and, after passing a lane on the left, we reach a level road that gives us another view over the reservoir on our right, complemented by a wonderful panorama of the Royal Bay of Grouville on our left. Below us we can see **Fort Henry**, among the fairways and greens of the the golf club. When we pass the church we will see the grave of seven men, stationed at Fort Henry, who fell fighting De Rullecourt's invasion force at La Rocque.

Soon this lane begins to descend, ahead on the skyline we can see the silhouette of Grouville Mill, whilst below and to the left stands the spire of Grouville Church. In the foreground is Grouville's expansive wetlands. This hill is quite steep and has a slippery green coating of moss in the middle. At the bottom it bends left and arrives suddenly at a yellow line, so be ready to brake. Here turn right and freewheel the last few yards to the valley floor. Cycle on past a tall tower built during the Occupation, that nowadays appears to be used for storing seed potatoes. Turn sharp right at the next turning, by now we have cycled 2.12 miles; 3.41 km. (**A**).

We are now on the other side of the valley and before long we draw level with the head of the dam. Climb a little further and the lane levels out. We reach a T-junction, where we turn left and then right. Some way along, where the lane meanders, amongst a stand of birch trees, we find a number of mallow plants. When we discover how soft their wide leaves are we instantly understand why they are found next to outside toilets!

Pass a cattle farm and turn left at the next yellow line. Cycle on, passing a turning on the left as we do so. Once again the sweep of Grouville Bay appears on our left. Take the first right to head inland. After the right hand bend, turn left immediately into a pleasant lane which gives a good view of the surrounding countryside and the little chapel on top of La Hougue Bie over to the right. The lane bends left, running parallel to a stream down on the right. The lane descends gently and we take the first turning on the right. We descend into a tranquil valley. This little lane is quite delightful, and it comes as no surprise to learn it won the Scenic Lanes Award in 1997. The plaque commemorating this can be seen at the yellow line, after we have ascended the short hill out of the valley.

At the yellow line, using care, turn right and some yards further on, turn left into what seems like a cart track. Bounce your way along the track, stop at the yellow line and turn left. Enjoy an easy freewheel for the next quarter of a mile. Pass a lane on the right and at the next junction turn right, but be careful as we are crossing the flow of traffic. The road bends left and we continue past a road entering from the right, until we reach a yellow line where we turn left. Bear right at the fork to arrive at a tiny crossroads. So far we have come 4.95 miles; 7.97 km. (**B**).

Following *Route 8*, cross straight over and continue on, taking the first left. This will take us up to a crossroads with the main road. Cross straight over and then straight on again at another set of crossroads soon after. The lane falls away slightly as we begin to return to sea level. We can see Mont Orgueil castle in the distance as the slope takes us along. The lane swings left and arrives abruptly at a T-junction. Turn right and descend the hill. Miss a discreet lane on the right and proceed on to the yellow line, which is just after a hill on the left. Here we need to turn right into **La Rue de Grouville**.

The road rises as we make our way to the church and the Parish Hall, passing a lane on the right that emerges from the woodland and another lane from the right further on. The road widens and meets **Grouville Hill** opposite the Parish Hall. Turn left here and cycle on towards the church, avoiding a hill adjacent to the Parish Hall. If time allows, dismount and enter the churchyard.

The largest tombstone near the road is that of seven grenadiers of the 83rd Regiment of Foot. These soldiers fell fighting Baron De Rullecourt's rearguard at La Rocque on January 6th 1781.

Mont Orgueil Castle and Gorey Harbour

Above: Lavoir at La Rue du Marais à La Cocque

Right: Pump at La Rue du Marais à La Cocque

Leave the church and turn into **La Route des Côtils**, which is the lane directly opposite the church. Again use caution as we cross the road. The lane bends to the left and then bends left again, after passing the foot of a small hill on the right. The road swings right and straightens up before we need to bear right at the fork. Cycle on in the shade of the trees. Before long the plain of Grouville appears before us. The road falls away and we arrive at a crossroads. Here at the end of La Route des Côtils, we have come 7.05 miles; 11.35 km. (**C**), we turn left.

> As we cycle along, look out for a white angular building on the right. This was Fauvic Station, when the railway ran between St. Helier and Gorey. The line of the track can be easily spotted on the other side of the road, where a tree-lined embankment crosses the marshy pasture.

Cycle on and, on meeting the main coast road at a T-junction, turn left and then left again to return on the other side of the marsh.

> Again it is possible to estimate the route of the railway as we look to the right when we reach the railway embankment. As we draw near to the next junction, an impressive pump set high on a pedestal is seen on our left. The pump, erected in 1930, sits alongside a beautifully crafted well and lavoir. The lavoir was ceded to the parish in 1999, and was restored as part of the Millennium celebrations. Here, turn right to head north and begin our return to Gorey. When the lane divides, bear right and, after passing a road from the right, take the next right. This little lane snakes right and left and we arrive at the **Grouville primary school**. The school looks extremely modern, even the oldest part is, by local standards quite new. An increase in pupils just before the Second World War forced the school to leave its original premises, now the Parish Hall, and a new school was built on this present site in 1939.

At the yellow line after the school turn left. Where we join a road that comes in at an angle, go straight on. Cycle on to the crossroads and go straight over into **La Cache des Pres**. In only a few yards we find ourselves in the midst of the wetlands. On the left, three streams advance towards us, and numerous shallow ponds litter the marsh on both sides of the road. The marsh is an ecological haven for many species, either as a permanent home or as a migratory stopover. It is not unusual to see teal, sand martins and sedge warblers here en route to different destinations.

Right: A Wetland Stream

Left: Prince of the Wetlands.

As we approach the end of the lane, change down and climb the short hill up to the junction. Turn right and head back towards the village. Depending on the season, the steeply sloping fields to the left may contain Jersey New Potatoes, planted during the first weeks of the year. Follow the smooth tarmac of this lane as it meanders along past a number of allotments, quite an unusual sight for Jersey and take the first right. Freewheel down towards the sea, and at the junction turn right. When we reach the main road turn left. Our starting point is about 400 yards along the road on the right.

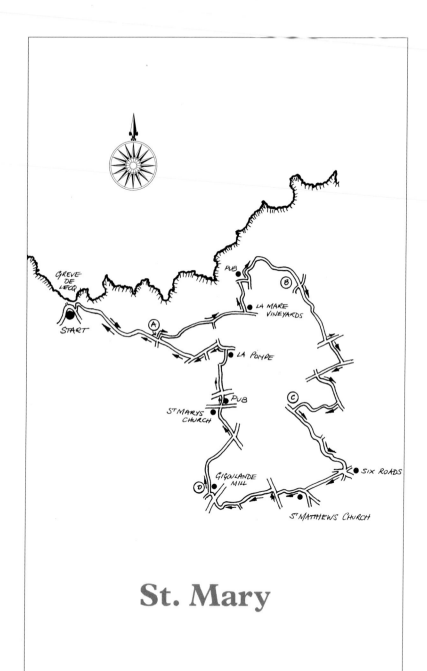

GREVE
DE
LECQ

PUB

START

A

B

LA MARE
VINEYARDS

LA POMPE

PUB

ST MARYS
CHURCH

C

GIGOULANDE
MILL

D

SIX ROADS

ST MATTHEWS CHURCH

St. Mary

St. Mary
Untouched by Time

This ride takes us to one of Jersey's truly rural parishes; St. Mary. Having the smallest number of postal addresses in the island, St. Mary certainly has more grass than granite.

Getting There: Approximate distance 8 Miles; 12.88 km.

Leave Jersey Tourism, and using the crossing, cross over towards the harbour. Having crossed over, turn right and head west towards St. Aubin.

Use care when crossing the odd section of roadway. If we are going in the right direction we will pass **The Grand Hotel** in around .55 mile; 0.89 km. Be ready to sound your bell here and there, as not everyone realises they are walking on a cycle track.

Continue along the track as it borders the sea wall. At Bel Royal, opposite the burger bar, we will have cycled 2.12 miles; 3.41 km. At 2.57 miles; 4.14 km., immediately after a small car park with white railings, turn right inland to pick up *Route 4*.

Cycle up the gravel path and on reaching tarmac turn left and then right into **Rue du Moulin**. At the main road turn right and left following *Route 4*, passing the Battle of Flowers headquarters on our left. Continue along this road as it bends left, avoiding a steep hill on the left, and take a hairpin right into the Green Lane, **Les Charrières de Malorey**. Climb the hill, passing Le Manoir de Malorey on your left and a minor road on the right. When the hill flattens out, miss a lane on the left and we soon arrive at a T-junction. Here take a left, following *Route 4* again. Carry straight on at the next crossroads adjacent to Morel Farm, by now we will have cycled 4.38 miles; 7.05 km.

At the next set of crossroads turn left, following *Route 3* towards St. Ouen's Bay. When the lane emerges opposite the church, at the end of **Rue des Bessieres**, turn right and bear left around the graveyard into **La Rue Bechervaise**. Following *Route 3*, turn right at the T-junction. However do not follow *Route 3* at the next turning but go straight ahead into **La Cheve Rue**. The lane descends, and when we emerge into the sunlight we pass **The Elms**, headquarters of The National Trust for Jersey.

Climb briefly up to the yellow line and, using care, turn right. At the top of the slope, when the road forks, bear left towards the church. At the yellow line at the end of **La Rue de la Vallee**, opposite the church we have cycled 6.17 miles; 9.93 km. Cross the main road into **La Rue de L'Eglise** and at the next crossroads turn left. Take the next right after **St. Mary's Primary School** into **La Rue du Pont**, passing the **Parish Hall**.

After passing a fine granite residence, turn left into **Le Hurel**. The lane falls away as we begin the descent towards our starting point in the bay. Turning left at the yellow line takes us to the junction with the main road. Here at the end of **La Charrière** we turn right.

Miss a lane on the right, and as we freewheel down, a sign on the granite wall on the right says **Le Mont de Ste Marie**. At the bottom of the hill, after the road levels out, continue on uphill for a short distance. Our starting point is in the tarmac car park on the left.

The Route: Approximate distance 10 miles; 16.09 km.

Our starting point is the sloping tarmac car park that overlooks **Grève de Lecq Bay**, the imposing Round Tower in the middle of the car park making it impossible to miss. The flat sandy beach of Grève de Lecq has always offered an attractive landing point for an enemy, and the various fortifications around the bay bear witness to this. This particular tower was one of the first three erected in the island, being built in 1780, a year after the Duke of Nassau's unsuccessful attack on the island in St. Ouen's Bay.

Leaving the car park turn right and freewheel towards the **Millennium Cross** which is situated at the foot of a steep hill that leads past the barracks. Turn sharp left here into **Le Chemin du Catel** and proceed up the hill, passing the barracks which have been restored by the National Trust and are open to the public

Ascend the hill and dismount at the blue *Route 1* sign. It is only relatively recently that cyclists have been allowed to walk up this hill against the flow of traffic, and it's only the super fit or foolhardy who would contemplate cycling up. Before the lane turns right, take a moment to enjoy the view over the bay: in the middle distance behind Café Casino stands a German bunker which once housed a 10.5 cm gun, the main armament of the bay. Just below us we can see the roof of another bunker, this one had a 7.5 cm gun. Both bunkers are of "Fortress" strength which means they are made of reinforced concrete two metres thick !. Unfortunately the pier, built in 1872, was not as substantial as it succumbed to the waves some 13 years later.

When the hill levels out, the large mound on your left is the remains of what is thought to be an Iron Age fort, still in use as late as the early 1400s, it was one of the five castles of refuge into which islanders would flee in times of hostility.

The route is predominately flat from now on, so remount and cycle on past **Crabbé Rifle Range** bearing to the right into **Rue du Crabbé**. Avoiding a right turning into a Green Lane, go a little further and turn left on *Route 1* into **La Rue des Touettes (A)**, having covered just over 1 mile; 1.61 km.

The lane bends right and depending on the visibility, we can see the other islands in the distance. The road rises and following *Route 1* we bear left.

Take the next left, and as we skirt the grounds of **La Mare Vineyard** we may be able to spot the miniature ponies "Bubble" and "Fizz". That is providing they have not made another escape. The road swings right and left and once again the islands come into view. Invariably we experience the cold north wind blowing into our face here, but we soon turn away and arrive at a yellow line where we take a left. The road winds itself behind the **Priory** public house, ascending into a Green Lane; **Le Chemin des Hougues**.

> Notice on the left, a Millennium Stone, one of twelve dotted around the parishes. Like the others, this one has a small plaque at the base explaining that it was erected by our local Territorial Army rather than by prehistoric man.

The road rises and begins its descent into **Le Mourier Valley**. Watch out for moss and gravel on the road here, and avoid any sudden manoevres. At the ruined cottages, the lane starts to climb gently and a very busy brook rushes past on our left. The fact that there were three water mills in this valley is borne out by the name of the house on the right, **L'Ecluse**, which means the mill pond. As we approach the junction we can hear streams gurgling away on both sides of the road.

At this crossroads (**B**), having cycled 3 miles; 4.83 km., we go straight over into a very shady and heavily wooded lane. The lush vegetation on the right-hand side being fed by another stream making its way down to the sea. The lane turns right and left through a group of houses, it rises and we come upon a road name at last, **La Rue D'enfer.**

At the end of this Green Lane we meet the main road, turn left here and exercising EXTREME CAUTION turn right into another Green Lane; **La Rue du Muet.** Enjoy the shade provided by this leafy lane, and at the T-junction turn right into **La Rue de Bel Air.**

Continue along this road and take the next left into **La Rue de Douet.** The word douet indicates a stream, and the road slopes as we freewheel toward the stream bed. At the bottom of the slope turn right into the bumpy lane which runs parallel to the stream. The abundance of bullrushes, reeds and cow parsley marks the path of the stream.

For a few yards we are in St. Lawrence, but as the lane winds right and left it crosses the stream again, and we return into St. Mary. As if to emphasize the point a clump of aurum lilies peek out from under a garden fence on the right. The lily has always been associated with the Virgin Mary, and St. Mary has the fleur de lys as its parish symbol. The lane bends right, climbs and eventually ends at a T-junction.

Here, at the end of the Green Lane, **La Rue de La Prairie,** (**C**) we have covered nearly 5 miles; 8.05 km., almost halfway. Turn left here onto the main road. The road bends left and right and becomes **Les Chanolles des Six Rues.** After following this road for about a quarter of a mile, a magnificent oak on the corner ahead signals our arrival into the hamlet of Six Roads.

Where the six roads meet, take the second from the right into **La Longue Rue.** Ahead of us we see the spire of St. Matthew's Catholic Church. At the yellow line in front of the church take a right into **Rue Bechervaise.** Miss a right turn, and continue through an S-bend, soon we arrive at a junction where we turn right following *Route 3*. This section of road may look familiar, we used it on our way out to the starting point. However this time, turn left opposite the farm, following the *Route 3* sign once again.

A chain link fence stretches ahead on the right, beyond it is the quarry workings of Granite Products. We pick up speed and when the blue cycle route signs appear, carry straight on into **Mont Remon**. The lane dives right and left, be ready to brake as the hill gets steeper as it draws closer to its junction with the main road.

Using caution, cross the main road into the lane ahead. If you cast a glance to your right, you can just see the remains of **Gigoulande Mill** in the shadows.

Gigoulande Mill was quite unusual as it had two water wheels, and was "overshot". That is to say the water fell from above, first onto the upper wheel, and then from that wheel onto the lower one.

The lane swings left, immediately turn right into **La Dimerie**, another Green Lane. (**D**) We have now covered 7 miles; 11.27 km. As the lane rises, we can see on our left the remains of The Fantastic Tropical Gardens, a popular tourist attraction not so long ago. A replica Model T Ford once used to promote the place now lies abandoned in the undergrowth.

We pass a water meadow on our left, and as the road starts to climb toward St.Mary's Church, it becomes **La Rue des Potirons**. At the yellow line turn sharp left. After half a mile or so, **St. Mary's Church** appears and we can freewheel down to the junction. We see from the different styles of masonry that the church has grown from the small Norman church that stood there in the 11th century.

Once again employing caution, cross over the main road into **La Rue de L'Eglise**. At the next crossroads, go straight ahead again into La Rue de L'Eglise. Where the road turns right, notice the lone column ahead, with the remains of a wayside cross perched on the top. Soon this lane becomes **La Rue de La Grange**, and it leads us under an impressive canopy of trees past La Pompe, the first house in the parish to have a water pump.

Going between two of the oldest buildings of this farmstead, we arrive at a yellow line and turn left, follow the lane as it swings right then turn left into **La Rue du Pont**.

The road meanders slightly and suddenly a beautiful thatched cottage comes into view. Continue along this lane and after passing a farmyard on the right, turn right into **La Rue de Crabbé**. The road here has the same rough surface as the lanes we find in St. Ouen.

After passing a right and a left turning, we enter the tunnel of fir trees which we encountered on our way out. Just before the rifle range the road bears left into **Le Chemin du Catel**. On our left the heavily wooded valley that leads down to the bay can be seen, while the Paternosters reef out to sea may be seen to the right of Le Catel earthwork as we descend back into Grève de Lecq.

Grève de Lecq
Barracks

This hill is very steep, as I'm sure you will remember, so if in any doubt please walk down. At the bottom of the hill turn right to return to our starting point in the car park.

St. Martin

Within sight of the sea

I have to confess that I break my vow of 'no hills' almost immediately on this excursion around my home parish of St. Martin. But I am sure that the view afforded the rider on reaching the summit will offset any effort involved.

Getting there: Approximate distance 8.25 miles; 13.28 km.

Leave **Liberation Square** and head north up **Conway Street**, which is just to the left of the **Pomme D'Or Hotel**. After 150 yards or so turn right into **Bond Street**. At the crossroads go straight over into **Pier Road** and ascend the hill. Once past the multi-storey car park on the left, bear left and climb a little further. Follow the road as it bends to the left and descends slightly beneath some trees. By the time we reach the next junction we will have come 0.7 miles; 1.13 km. Turn left and descend the hill, continuing straight on ahead past hotels and in due course the **Bathing Pool**.

After passing the Bathing Pool we arrive at a roundabout. Here we have to give way to traffic coming from the right, so, when the road is clear, turn right. Follow this road for a short distance and then bear left into **Green Road**. At the traffic lights we have cycled 1.60 miles; 2.58 km. Turn left and cycle on to the bend ahead. Where the road bends to the left, using care, turn right into **La Blinerie**, a Green Lane. Follow this pleasant lane past the golf course and take the first left. As soon as the lane has turned sharp left, turn right at the foot of a hill, following *Route 1*. Climb the hill and turn right at the tiny crossroads halfway up. Climb a

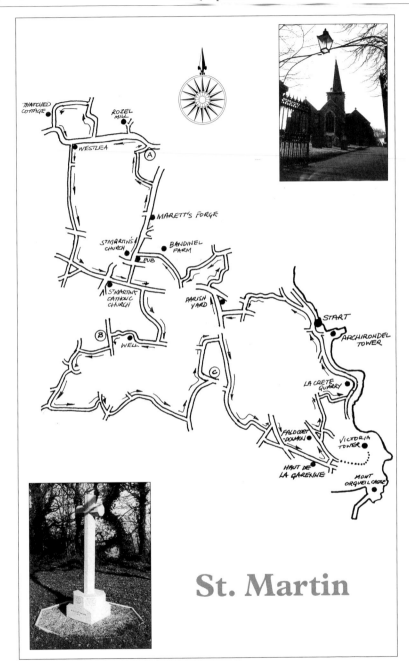

THATCHED COTTAGE

ROZEL MILL

WESTLEA

A

MARETT'S FORGE

ST MARTIN'S CHURCH

BANDINEL FARM

PUB

ST MARTIN'S CATHOLIC CHURCH

PARISH YARD

B

WELL

C

START

ARCHIRONDEL TOWER

LA CRETE QUARRY

FALDOUET DOLMEN

VICTORIA TOWER

HAUT DE LA GARENNE

MONT ORGUEIL CASTLE

St. Martin

little further until we reach a yellow line where we turn left. Continue on to the yellow line at the end of this road. Here, at the end of **Rue au Blancq**, we meet the main road at the top of Grouville Hill. By now we have cycled 3.56 miles; 5.73 km.

Leave the yellow line and turn right to descend the hill for a short distance. Just after the **Millennium Cross**, take a left and follow *Route 8*. At the crossroads turn left to freewheel down to a T-junction where we turn right. The lane snakes right and left and we arrive at a small crossroads. By now we have cycled 4.28 miles; 6.89 km.

Go straight over. At the next yellow line turn left and then right very soon after. We pass a row of greenhouses and a lane that comes in from the left, before the road bends to the right and, arrives quite suddenly at a yellow line. Turn left and continue along this lane missing a little lane on the left, but taking the second right into a lane that comes in at an angle. Follow this short stretch of tarmac until we reach a crossroads where we turn left. At the next junction, opposite **La Hougue Bie**, turn right and cycle up to the yellow line.

Here cross into **Rue Champ Colin** and begin to follow *Route 3*. We can freewheel along this lane for a while. When the lane bends right continue straight on into **Rue de Neuilly**. Again we can freewheel until reaching a yellow line where we turn sharp right. Cycle through a crossroads into **Rue St. Julien**. Miss a lane on the left and, at the T-junction, turn left and climb a slight rise. At the top of **Rue de la Chouquetterie** we have come 6.95 miles; 11.19 km. Here turn left to join *Route 1* for a very short time.

The lane bends to the right. Miss a lane on the left and, after the lane bends right again, we arrive at a yellow line. Here at the end of **Rue du Bouillon** turn left and, when we meet the main road at the crossroads, go straight over and take the first right. Follow this road through a crossroads and miss a left at the top of the hill before descending. This long hill bends left as it makes its way down and, just before reaching the yellow line, we pass a lane on the left. At the junction at the bottom turn left and soon after turn right into the small gravel car park.

The Route*: Approximate distance 10 miles; 16.09 km.*

This route starts in the gravel car park at the southern end of the **Pine Walk**, near Archirondel. Leaving the car park, we turn right toward the Pine Walk, but almost immediately fork left up a slight incline, **Rue des Viviers**, which steepens as we progress. Keep left when the road divides at the granite date stone. The rider is best advised to walk up this hill, and enjoy the canopy of vegetation that shades the road. This road is literally a 'Green Lane', because little traffic allows moss to grow on the tarmac . We will see two more of these green lanes on our route today.

When the hill levels out, the presence of fuchsia and roses on both sides of the road gives you the impression that you are in someone's garden.

> To your right the whole length of St. Catherine's Breakwater can be seen, together with Gibraltar, the mound created by the quarrying of granite for the breakwater. The breakwater was built between 1847 and 1854 as part of a huge harbour to house the British Fleet. The other longer arm was to run from Archirondel, near our starting point, out to the beacon in the bay. Why the project was never completed is open to debate. Certainly by the time the breakwater was complete, relations with France were on a stable footing and a naval presence so close to the French coast would have not been acceptable. In essence though, the depth of water in the bay was never sufficient for such ships, and this was something that was overlooked at the project's inception.

Press on up the hill and, after the lane bends left, miss a lane on the right. When we reach the crossroads at the end of **Rue des Ormes** turn right and then right again at the following T-junction. Once past the junction we can see the coast of France and the Ecréhous on our right over the hedge. As we near the next yellow line we pass St. Martin's parish yard. We may find several heaps of soil in front of this building; these are piles of road sweepings called *bannelais* which are sold annually at auction and then used as a natural fertiliser by the farmers.

Cross the yellow line and, being careful, go almost straight ahead into **La Verte Rue**. As the road twists and turns, the breakwater comes into view again. Turn left at the next yellow line, the road climbs slightly and after passing a lane on the right, the spire of St. Martin's Church and the roof tops of the village appear on the horizon. When **Rue de la Forge** ends at the yellow line turn right. The lane dips and rises again.

At the corner take time to admire a fine example of a Jersey farmhouse; **Bandinel Farm**. David Bandinel was the first Anglican Dean of Jersey. In 1645, Bandinel and his son James, the Rector of St. Mary, were incarcerated in Mont Orgueil for their anti-Royalist views. It was whilst trying to escape from the castle that Bandinel fell to his death.

A tunnel of trees shields us from the elements as we head towards the Parish Church. At the T-junction at the end of **La Chasse des Demoiselles Bandinel** turn right, but exercise care as it is impossible to see traffic coming from the right. Freewheel down the hill, passing two lanes on the right at the bottom. The road climbs slightly and just before the crest we find **Marett's Forge**.

Once past the forge we can coast down a gentle slope, passing a lane on the left at the brow, before taking a left into **Rue de la Pallotterie**. Take care in this lane, as once again lack of use gives it a coating of slippery green moss. In the light of the valley we find a pumping station and a clump of bamboo before we climb out. This is the last steep hill we will encounter and I suggest walking up, as these routes were never intended as a physical challenge.

At the yellow line, opposite a house called **Haute Entrée**, (**A**) we have come 2.66 miles; 4.28 km. Here turn left. After passing a group of houses on the left, a view of trees, fields and valleys can be seen stretching back to the church. If we take the next right, we will see the tall structure of **Rozel Mill**. This was one of only two mills in the parish, the other being a water mill near St. Catherine's crossroads. Like many wind mills it was used as an observation post by the Germans in the last war.

Return to the road we left and turn right following our original course. After about 200 yards, turn right into **Rue des Huriaux**. This lane gives fabulous views of the coast of France and the Ecréhous. In fact after meandering left, right and left again, the road rises slightly and a panorama of France, the sea and the intervening farm land presents itself. The lane becomes **Rue du Rat** and it dips and climbs once more.

St. Catherine's Breakwater

On our right is a very attractive thatched cottage with a peacock strutting along the ridge of the roof. This house has only been rethatched in the past few years, previously it had a corrugated iron roof. This house is one of four thatched houses on the island, and though it seems an old fashioned method of roofing, modern thatch can easily last a hundred years.

Continue on to the next junction, at the end of what is now **Rue de la Ville Bree**. Turn left here and then right immediately after a bend in the road. On the left is **Westlea**, a private house converted to a centre for the blind in 1994. The paving stones outside the building have different surfaces to assist the residents in making their way about.

A gentle slope allows us a brief rest as we pass a lane on the left, and some way further on cross another 'bridge'. The stream it crosses is the same one we met in Rue de la Palloterie. It eventually runs out into the sea at St.Catherine and used to provide the power for the parish water mill.

Go over the crossroads, on our left we see the houses and church of the village again. Take the first left into **Rue de la Mare des Reines**, miss a right, and go through the next crossroads into **La Longue Rue**.

> On the right is St. Martin's Catholic Church built in 1862 to accommodate the large number of French and Irish residents in the parish. Behind the church lies the grave of Colonel Charles Edward Stuart, who believed himself to be the great grandson of Bonnie Prince Charlie, and therefore heir to the throne.

Pass a lane on the left and take the next right into **Rue de L'Orme**. The lane winds until we reach a T-junction where we turn right. Follow the road and as it twists and turns look out for a well head on the left of the road, just past what appears to be a two-storey high nissen hut.

When **Rue de la Fontaine** ends, turn left. At this point we have cycled 5.63 miles; 9.06 km. (**B**). Freewheel for a few yards before taking a right turn into **Rue de Benjamin**. Opposite the granite pumping station turn left. Forty years ago a row of chestnut trees graced this lane and a stream ran in a culvert beneath them. Turn left, then right immediately into **Rue Champ Colin**.

Continue on, avoiding a lane on the right, and take a left into **Rue de Neuilly**. At the yellow line turn sharp right and as the lane descends carry straight on between two buildings into **Rue St. Julien**. Miss a hill that comes in from the left. For about two hundred yards we are actually in St. Saviour. The stream which was originally on our right has crept under the road and we have slipped into the neighbouring parish. At the junction turn left. As we climb we see two wooden huts, relics of the Occupation, but nevertheless still used as dwellings until fairly recently.

At the top of **Rue de la Chouquetterie (C)** turn left again. By now we will have come 7.54 miles; 12.13 km. Follow the road as it bends right and continue on, passing a lane on the left. The lane bends once more and arrives at a T-junction, just after passing a pair of very old granite doorways facing each other across the tarmac. Turn right and coast for a while as we head back towards the sea, passing a road on the right as we do so.

When we reach the main road turn left and then right at the yellow line, going towards Gorey. Before the road starts to descend, turn left into **Rue de la Pouclée et des Quatre Chemins**.

> Once again the sea comes into view on our right, the full sweep of the Royal Bay of Grouville as far as La Rocque Tower can be seen. A little further on stands **Haute de La Garenne**, famous as the 'Bureau des Etrangers' in the television series Bergerac. Rather than continuing around to the left, detour a moment and go straight ahead down a slope towards the sea. A magnificent perspective of **Mont Orgueil** with the harbour below stands before us. The castle was built around 1204, when King John lost his lands in France, and the island suddenly became an outpost of his kingdom. The advent of gunpowder heralded the castle's demise, as its position facing Mont St.Nicholas put it within cannon range.

Return to our original route and, after passing a right turn, we pass the **Faldouet Dolmen** on the left.

> First recorded in 1682, this dolmen is the most southerly in the British Isles and the impressive 23 ton rhyolite capstone remains in its original position over the main burial chamber.

Take the right turn after the dolmen. At the yellow line turn left and rather than descending to the right, keep left as the lane climbs slightly as we skirt the heights above Anne Port.

> When the road levels out, stop and look over your right shoulder and you will see **Victoria Tower**. Built in 1837, it is one of eight English style towers in the island and has the distinction of being the last Martello Tower built in Europe.

Victoria Tower, 1837 (left); Archirondel Tower and Battery (right)

Continue along and take the lane that comes in on the right; **Mont de la Crete**. This is the third and final 'green lane', and as it is both steep and slippery I suggest anyone who doubts their cycling skills should DISMOUNT AND WALK. Your patience will be rewarded by a superb outlook over Anne Port from an unusual angle.

Descend down to the yellow line. After turning left, return along the coast road.

As we round the corner opposite La Crete quarry, we see the Jersey Round Tower at Archirondel and the unfinished stub of the southern arm of the harbour. The tower is actually built on an island, the gap between it and the land being filled in. It was the penultimate tower to be built and, like La Rocco in St. Ouen's Bay, it has a gun battery around its base.

Pass a lane that enters from the left and then the bottom of **Les Landes Hill** to return to the start.

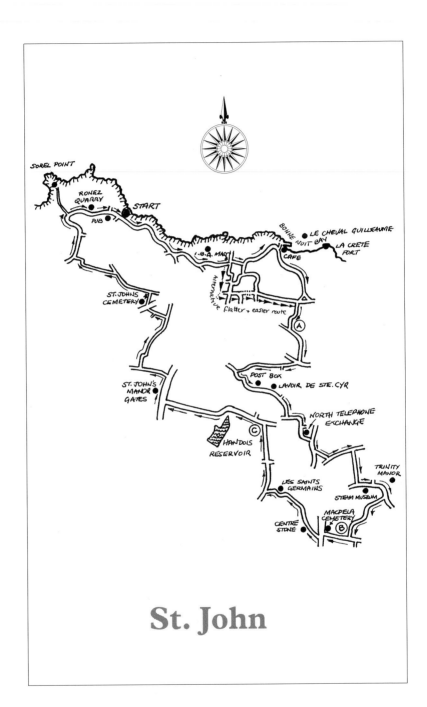

SOREL POINT

RONEZ QUARRY

PUB

START

LE CHEVAL GUILLEAUME

BONNE NUIT BAY

LA CRETE FORT

I.B.A. MAST

CAFE

Alternative flatter + easier route

ST. JOHNS CEMETERY

(A)

POST BOX

LAVOIR DE STE. CYR

ST. JOHN'S MANOR GATES

NORTH TELEPHONE EXCHANGE

HAN'DOIS RESERVOIR

(C)

TRINITY MANOR

LES SAINTS GERMAINS

STEAM MUSEUM

MACPELA CEMETERY

CENTRE STONE

(B)

St. John

St. John

From sea to centre stone

St. John is a parish with a diverse range of scenery. From the rugged cliffs of its north coast to its borders with St.Helier in the south, we will see a little of everything Jersey can offer. The coastline is punctuated by small coves and harbours, causing the coastal road to climb and dive in unison. As we travel south, we have the gradient in our favour and we cross streams as they hurry to the sea.

Getting there: Approximate distance 8.25 miles; 13.28 km.

Leave **Liberation Square** and, using the crossing, cross over to the quayside. Turn right and proceed west, parallel to the road. Climb the rise and, using care, cross the two roads that go to the Elizabeth Terminal. Continue on a gravel track, crossing the car park slip road, until we reach the granite paving. Here we are able to pick up the white markings of the cycle track.

The single white line becomes two lines and we follow these towards the far end of the bay. We will pass the **Old Station Café** in 1.75 miles; 2.82 km. and leave the track at the small car park with the white railings in 2.57 miles; 4.14 km. Here we turn right and follow *Route 4* inland.

Using the crossing, cross over into a gravel path. Cycle up this track and, when we reach the road, turn left and immediately right following *Route 4*, into **Rue du Moulin**. At the junction with the main valley road turn right and then immediately left, where **Tesson Chapel** makes the corner. This road is **La Rue des Pres**

Sorsoleil. Pass the Battle of Flowers Association building and, avoiding a steep hill on the left, bear left and then take a hairpin right into the Green Lane, **Les Charrieres de Malorey**. Ascend the hill, missing a lane on the right, and further on a lane coming in from the left. Continue up to a T-junction, here turn left following *Route 4*. At the next crossroads, where Les Charrieres de Malorey becomes **Rue Rouge Cul**, we have come 4.38 miles; 7.05 km. Proceed ahead.

At the next crossroads where the Green Lane ends, go straight over on *Route 4* towards St .John's Village and then next right into **La Ruette D'Avranches**. Follow the lane as it bends and leads us to the main road, passing a pump, as it does so. At the yellow line, carefully cross almost straight over into a narrow Green Lane.

At the end of this little lane, **La Ruette**, turn right and immediately left into **La Rue du Douet de Rue**, again following the signs for *Route 4*. The lane swings left and right and begins a lazy descent. Miss a left and then a right turning and continue on under a canopy of trees. When we reach the bottom of the slope avoid a lane on the left and climb the shallow hill ahead, **La Rue du Douet**. The road bends left and right and arrives at a crossroads. We have cycled 6.06 miles; 9.75 km. so far. Here, turn right and continue past two left turns.

At the third turning on the left, turn into **Rue des Buttes**, a Green Lane. Cycle up this inviting lane and continue on towards the church, avoiding a lane on the left, until we reach the yellow line adjacent to the parish hall. Cross over to go between the church and the pub and follow the road as it bends right between the shops. At the yellow line after the shops, turn left onto *Route 1*.

Go straight over the next crossroads into **Rue de L'Etocquet**, and after 300 yards or so, take the first right into the Green Lane; **La Rue des Landes**. Miss a very small lane on the right and continue on as the lane begins to descend. When we arrive at a T-junction turn right. Freewheel down, missing a Green Lane on the left. The lane bends right and left and emerges at a yellow line. Cross over into the large tarmac car park to arrive at our starting point for St. John.

The Route: Approximate distance 10.5 miles; 16.9 km.

We start our ride in the large tarmac car park on the **New North Road**, just across from the public house.

> As we can gather from the memorial stone in the car park, this road was built during the war. Initially planned to run from Le Mourier Valley to Gorey, it was built using a local labour force, as over 2000 men had been made redundant due to the island's occupation by the Germans. In actual fact, only the stretch from Sorel to La Saline was ever built.

Leave the car park and turn left in the direction of the huge mast on the skyline ahead. On a fine day we will see the coast of France on our left. This well maintained road swerves left and right as it follows the cliff's edge. Continue on **La Rue du Nord** as it bends left, passing the **St. John's Millennium Cross**, and avoiding two roads that come in from the right. The road drops as we pass a granite recycling works on the right. Here old granite is dressed ready for re-use in the island's pavements. Soon a steady but testing climb takes us out of La Rue du Nord and left into **La Rue es Nonnes**.

> At the end of the local cycle racing calendar, it is customary to have a fun event which starts in this very lane. It is the annual freewheel competition. Competitors have their pedal cranks strapped to the bicycle's frame, so that they are unable to pedal. They are positioned at the top of the hill that we have just climbed, and then released. The rider that freewheels the farthest is the winner! I remember someone actually getting as far as our starting point, though I believe it was achieved by a now outlawed technique. As a rough guide the heaviest rider usually wins.

A few yards further on we pass the Independant Broadcasting Authority transmitter, this is the massive radio mast on the left.

At the end of this lane we get a preview of the sea and cliffs ahead in the distance. Here we have a choice of routes; either a drop into the little harbour of Bonne Nuit and a climb of one of the most challenging hills in the island, or a detour on flatter roads to rejoin the route again at the top of the climb.

If choosing the easier route, turn right at this yellow line and follow the road as it winds left and right through an S-bend. Continue on past a right and then a left turning until we arrive at a small crossroads. At this crossroads turn left into **La Ruette de la Carriere**, which is on *Route 1* of the cycle network. Ascend this hill and, rather than following the tarmac at the bend, go straight on into a narrow gravel track called **Mont Mado Lane**. Take care as the lane is probably overgrown. On our left, what is now grassed over was once Mont Mado Quarries, famous for the quality of its granite. On reaching the end of this rough track, cross straight over what is in effect a crossroads. The road slopes away and we need to take the first right into **La Rue des Chaigniers**. We are now back on our original route.

If prefering the hilly option, turn left at the yellow line and then right into **La Rue de la Lande**. Where this short lane meets the main hill turn left. We begin the steep descent into Bonne Nuit Bay.

After a sharp right turn, the road meanders slightly and begins to climb almost immediately. If we turn left before the hill rises, it will take us to the bay and the harbour.

The hill climbs steadily for nearly half a mile, gaining around 400 feet in altitude as it does so, and getting steeper as it nears the summit!. Bearing this in mind it is probably wise to walk at least some of the way.

> As we begin the ascent, take the opportunity to admire the view of the small harbour, and **La Crete**, a Napoleonic fort at the far end of the bay. This is now used as a summer residence for the Lieutenant Governor, the Queen's representative in the island. Also notice the rocky outcrop in the middle of the bay, this is known as **Le Cheval Guilleaume**, following a legend which grew up around it. A wicked sea sprite had fallen in love with a girl from the area, but she was already in love with a young soldier called Guilleaume. In an effort to dispose of Guilleaume, the sprite turned himself into a stunning white charger which Guilleaume found in his stable just before he departed again for the wars. Thinking it was a present from his girlfriend, he rode down to the beach at Bonne Nuit expecting to see her. As he neared the water, the sprite seized his chance and galloped headlong into the sea, hoping to drown Guilleaume as he clung on to the bridle. Guilleaume, sensing his fate, let go of the horse and swam back to shore; whilst the sprite, his magic now exhausted, turned into the rock we see before us.

Just before the summit, bear right for a short distance to a yellow line, where we turn right. In a few yards turn left into **La Rue des Chataigniers**.

> It may be encouraging to discover that the hill that we have just climbed is used annually for competitive cycle hillclimbs, however the start is near the pier and the finish is some 200 yards further up!

This lane swings right and left and we arrive at a T-junction (**A**), if we took the Bonne Nuit route earlier, we will have covered 2.3 miles; 3.7 km. At the end of **La Rue des Chataigniers** turn left, and follow the road as it bends right and finally meets the main road at the stepped crossroads. Using care, leave **La Rue du Mont Mado**, and cross over to begin a long easy freewheel into the heart of the parish. Miss a left turn, and at the next yellow line turn left. This road climbs slightly and after an S-bend descends again.

What I believe is the smallest postbox in the island can be found in the granite wall of the building on the left. I see from the cypher that it was put up in the reign of Edward VII, which was between 1901 and 1910.

Freewheel some way further on, notice the large lavoir on the left, just before we cross the stream.

This is the Lavoir de St. Cyr, one of the best examples of a lavoir to be found in Jersey. This was a place for washing clothes, and a list of people allowed to use it can be seen on a tablet set into the wall on the left.

As we leave the lavoir the road climbs and bends. Miss a left turn and cycle a little further to a T-junction. Here we leave **Les Chenolles**, and turn left into **Le Chemin de Herupe**. The road bends to the right and missing a left, we continue on to the yellow line. The square building that we pass on the left was the North Telephone Exchange, one of the old manually operated telephone exchanges.

On reaching the main road, turn right and proceed along it for about 150 yards, then bear left into **La Rue de la Croix**. At the end of this lane turn left and head east. In a pedal stroke or two we will be in Trinity. The parish border is situated between two road name plates, both say 'La Rue de la Chesnaie', although they are on opposite sides of the road and of course in different parishes.

The road rises slightly and we take the first right into **La Neuve Route**. At the yellow line turn left and proceed past the Steam Museum and The Young Farmers Club, going from **La Rue de Bechet** into **La Rue du Brabant**.Miss a left turning and follow the road around a right hand bend, passing Trinity Manor on the left. After a slight left curve, turn right into **Rue des Canons**. Follow this lane as it dips and curves over a stream, and before long we see a road sign ahead that says **La Rue du Poivre**. Once in this lane we are back in St. John. Look out for the small cross of St. John on the road sign. At the yellow line at the end of La Rue du Poivre (**B**), we will have cycled 5.50 miles; 8.85 km.

> Turn right and head west. The lane twists and a cemetery appears ahead. This is **Macpela Cemetery** where we will find the graves of several political refugees who fled here in the 19th century. As most were either anarchists or aetheists, St. Helier was not keen to have them buried in the parish, so we find them here just outside St. Helier. In those days it would have been normal for all the refugees to follow the cortege up here, and occasionally for Victor Hugo, himself an exile here, to give a speech at the graveside.

Leave the cemetery, cross the main road, and bearing slightly left enter **La Rue des Servais**. This is on *Route 3* of the cycle network. We are literally in the middle of the island, as a house on the left called **Centre House** will verify. A little way beyond Centre House we pass a small granite cottage. Just behind it, partially submerged in the ground is a huge boulder. This is the centre stone, and is reputedly the centre of the island.

Freewheel on and La Rue des Servais becomes **La Rue des Saints Germains**, as we cross another stream and enter St. Lawrence.

> What I take to be an abreuvoir, a place to water cattle, can be seen on the stream bed on the right of the road. The fine dwelling of Les Saints Germains is on our right as the lane rises. This house was the home of the seigneur of Les Saints Germains, who had land in St.John, St.Saviour and St.Ouen, as well as in St.Lawrence. All these lands were considered as one, and called the fief de Saint Germain.

The lane bends left and right as it skirts the property. At the next junction we turn right and cycle north on *Route 3*. We pass through a crossroads as we go from **La Rue de St. Jean** into **La Rue du Bel au Vent**. A quaint direction sign marks the corner of the crossroads. We are on somewhat of a ridge here, and the fields on either side appear lower than the roadway.

When we meet the yellow line at the end of **La Rue du Bel au Vent (C)**, we will have cycled 7 miles; 11.27 km. Turn left into **Le Chemin de Herupe**. Go past a right hand turning, the road rises slightly and becomes **Le Hucquet**. We descend again into a shallow valley.

> This is the head of Waterworks Valley, and the reservoir that we see on our left is **Handois Reservoir**. Built in 1932, on the site of the old China Clay Quarries, Handois has a capacity of 187.5M litres. Ascend the small slope and continue along this lane until we meet the main road.

Turn right and cycle along **La Rue de la Mare Ballam**, passing the magnificent gates of St. John's Manor on the left. Take the next left into **Le Neuf Chemin**. This lane runs parallel to the manor's drive, in fact we turn off right into the Green Lane, **La Rue des Buttes**, before we reach the manor house, so long is the oak lined drive.

La Rue des Buttes is a charming lane. At its far end the lane goes through a tunnel of sycamore and chestnut. St. John's church and village lie ahead, so feel free to make a detour for refreshments, otherwise turn left into **La Rue Gombrette**. Cycle past a left turning and proceed on to the main road. At this yellow line, cross straight over into **La Rue du Cimetière**.

As we would expect, this lane runs beside the parish cemetery. What is unusual is the cemetery wall; it has a number of marriage stones set into it. Judging by their dates and designs they seem to come from a wide variety of sources. Before leaving the cemetery, look through the gates and see the impressive black marble gravestone of former parish resident and benefactor Sir Billy Butlin.

Continue on to the next junction and turn left. Follow this lane for some distance and, where it divides, bear left into a road called **Le Canibut**. The road bends right and left and a Green Lane sign appears on the left, using care turn right just after the sign. Follow this Green Lane, but rather than taking the first right on *Route 1*, proceed ahead around a left hand bend. The road bends right and we ascend **La Rue du Nord**. If we wish we can turn left here and follow the road to Sorel Point, where we will get an excellent view of the rugged north coast, the other islands and the rock face of Ronez Quarry.

Following **La Rue du Nord**, we pass the quarry entrance, and on reaching the top of the hill, a short freewheel takes us back to the start.

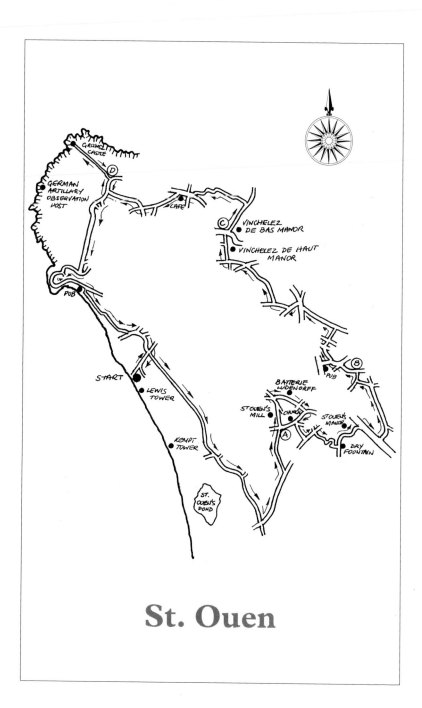

St. Ouen

St. Ouen

A Ride on the Wild Side

Our ride takes us way out west to St. Ouen, the island's biggest parish. The large amount of dune and heathland in St. Ouen means that we will see a landscape that has changed little during the course of time. Our route starts in the public car park at the north end of the Five Mile Road, near Les Laveurs Slip.

Getting there*:* Approximate distance 8.42 miles; 13.55 km.

Leave **Liberation Square** and cross the dual carriageway. Turn right at the quayside to head west. Cross the two roads that lead to the Elizabeth Terminal and continue along the gravel track to reach the marked cycle track by the granite seawall.

Follow the track past the Jersey Round Tower at **First Tower**, which we pass in 1.31 miles; 2.11 km. and the burger bar in 2.12 miles; 3.41 km. At the small car park, just beyond the burger bar, turn right to follow *Route 4* of the cycle network. Here we will have covered 2.57 miles; 4.14.km.

Use the crossing and proceed up the gravel path. At the end of the track, where it meets the road, turn left and continue straight ahead, past a right and a left turn, to begin to climb the Green Lane; **Les Grupieaux**. Once the lane has levelled out, Les Grupieaux becomes **Rue de la Fontaine**, passing a left turn as it does so and then a right turn some way further on.

At the yellow line at the end of **Rue de la Fontaine**, where it meets **Mont Fallu**, we have cycled 4.10 miles; 6.6 km. Cross the crossroads to go into the Green Lane. The next crossroads are in our favour, so go straight through again. Take the next left, at a stepped crossroads, into **Route du Manoir** and head towards the church steeple. From where we turned on to *Route 4* at the car park until now we have been cycling on the original Green Lane route which was opened in 1994.

At the yellow line, cross over to enter the village. Cycle through the village, going through a crossroads and missing a left just before the primary school. Opposite the school, turn right into **Rue de Bocage**, following *Route 6*. When we reach a crossroads cycle over, going from Rue de Bocage into **Rue des Niemes**. At the next crossroads turn left into **Rue de la Presse**. If we look over to the right, we see the white tower of St. Ouen's Mill and the spire of St. Ouen's Church, both of which are on our ride today.

Pass a lane on the left and soon the lane begins to descend. The lane forks, here bear left and remain on tarmac, avoiding the gravel Green Lane on the right. Soon we arrive at the yellow line at the end of **Rue de la Mont de la Mare**, bear right and descend further towards St. Ouen's Bay. The lane forks again, and again we must bear left and stay on the tarmac. At the bottom of the hill, **Mont de la Mare**, we have come 6.34 miles; 10.2 km. Turn right towards the little Methodist Chapel.

Go past the chapel and under the German railway bridge. Pass the head of Val de la Mare reservoir, the road rises and we go from **Rue du Moulin** over a crossroads. The lane ahead is very flat and easy to cycle on. Miss a small hill on the right and the lane swings left and right. We pass a lane on the right and one on the left, as the lane changes from **Val de la Mare** into **Chemin du Moulin**. We stay on this level lane for some distance, until we get to the crossroads at the end of Chemin du Moulin. Here we can turn left and freewheel towards the sea. At the bend, use care and go straight on to reach our starting point in the gravel car park on the left.

The Route: Approximate distance 12.3 miles; 19.79 km.

From the car park return toward the junction and continue up a slight rise, **La Route des Laveurs**, until we turn right at the crossroads into **Le Chemin du Moulin**. This lane led to the watermill Le Moulin de la Mare, which was situated where the head of Val de la Mare Reservoir is today, and which was powered by the stream which divides St. Ouen from St. Peter.

As we travel past **La Mielle de Morville** on our right, it is hard to believe that at one time this was an important area for dumping butchers' waste and other unsavoury rubbish. In 1979 the whole area was tidied up, contoured and planted with marram grass. It is now home to 400 species of wild flower. Close inspection reveals a whole carpet of tiny plants. These owe their existence to the humble rabbit, who by keeping the grass short, allows them to thrive.

The mild Jersey climate nurtures several plants and animals that are normally found nearer the Mediterranean, for example the Green Lizard, a creature that was marooned here during the Ice Age.

Press straight on as Chemin du Moulin becomes **Val de la Mare**. After the road winds left and right and passes a hill on the left, we reach a house called **Pond View**, on the left of the road. From this vantage point, we are able to see the whole panorama of the bay from Corbière Lighthouse at the far left to the rocky outcrop at L'Etacq on the right.

> La Mare au Seigneur, or **St.Ouen's Pond** is the largest natural expanse of freshwater in the Channel Islands. Throughout the year it is home to mallards and moorhens, whilst the Winter months sees migrant birds like shovelers and tufted ducks on its surface.

Continue along this road until the crossroads, where we turn left onto **Mont Rossignol**. This is the only long hill on our route, but it is not too steep. If you find it difficult, walk up and save your energies for later.

At the top, take the lane that branches off to the left, **Rue de la Campagne**.

> **St. Ouen's Mill**, Le Moulin de la Campagne, appears in front of us with the spire of St.Ouen's Church to the right. As we make our way towards the mill, notice the fields on the right. These are still cultivated as strip farming, a system used in the Middle Ages.

We reach the yellow line at the end of Rue de la Campagne (**A**) in 2.79 miles; 4.49 km. Here bear right and then left into the Green Lane ahead. Once past the mill, leave **Rue du Couvent** and take the second on the right into **Rue de la Cour**. We are now heading back towards the church and the hamlet that surrounds it.

> As we proceed up this lane, look over to the left, in front of Leoville rifle range, the low grey building, stands the remains of **Batterie Ludendorff**, a battery of three 210 mm guns assembled here during the Occupation. The side of a bunker can be seen beneath weeds and brambles on the left of the lane, with another in the field which makes the corner on the left.

Go through a crossroads and turn right into **Ville de L'Eglise** at the next yellow line. After passing through the village, turn left opposite the church and take the right fork into **La Rue**. When we meet **Mont Rossignol** again, turn left and then right at a small crossroads, a short distance further on. The lane dips and twists as it descends into a beautiful wooded valley. As you climb out, listen for the chorus of birdsong coming from the trees on both sides of the road.

Opposite the T-junction at the top stands another of those splendid Victorian edifices celebrating the parish officials of the time. In this instance, the Roads' Committee of 1898. This one was apparently a fountain, though not now working. Here turn left.

St. Ouen's Church

The dry fountain

As the road climbs, we catch sight of **St. Ouen's Manor** on the left.

The history of the manor can be traced back as far as 933, when William Longsword annexed the Channel Islands for the Duchy of Normandy. My favourite tale relates how Philippe de Carteret escaped capture from the island's French overlords by jumping a twenty foot wide ditch on his horse. The effort caused the valiant animal to expire, but not before delivering de Carteret safely back to the manor. De Carteret, realising that the horse had saved his life, had him buried in the grounds. Quite a story, especially as the ancient shoulder blade of a horse was dug up in the manor grounds at the turn of the 20th.century!

Rue du Coin becomes **Rue Vegueur** and before long we reach the entrance to the manor. Turn right onto the main road, and travel down it for 300 yards. Do take care here as the road is always busy.

Take the first left into **La Verte Rue**. As we make our way along this lane the telecommunication masts near St.Ouen's Village loom in the distance. This lane makes the parish boundary between St. Ouen and St. Peter, the fields on our right being in St.Peter. Miss a right and, at the yellow line turn left, then right at the next junction.

When we reach the end of **La Rue du Douet** (**B**), having cycled 5.28 miles; 8.5 km, turn left into **Rue de la Botellerie**, heading towards the tower of the Parish Hall. Go straight ahead over the next yellow line and cycle for a short distance along **Rue de la Forge**, before taking the first right into **Rue des Marettes**. This road will lead us through the heart of the modern village. Cycle on, missing a NO ENTRY on the left and a turning on the right, until we reach a crossroads. Cross over into the Green Lane ahead.

The sea comes into view as we approach a T-junction. Here we leave **La Verte Rue** and turn left into **Rue de la Capelle**. On reaching the main road, using care, turn right and then immediately left into **La Crosierie**. Continue along this road, taking the right fork onto the rough surface of **Rue de L'Etocquet**. Avoiding a lane on the left, follow this road as it sweeps right. Pass through the next crossroads, and miss a side road on the left. Take the next right into **Les Doubles Chasses**, miss a lane on the left and, as we enjoy another slope in our favour, the Manor of **Vinchelez de Haut** can be seen on the right. Just beyond it, on the far side of the road, lies the manor of **Vinchelez de Bas**. The fief of Vinchelez was split between the seigneur's two sons upon his death, and it is this that accounts for the two manors being so close together. Here, at the end of Les Doubles Chasses (**C**), we will have covered 7.28 miles; 11.72km.

Taking care, turn right at the yellow line and then almost immediately turn left into **Rue de Geonnais**. The grounds of Vinchelez de Bas Manor are on our right. What appears to be the base of a wayside cross rests on the manor wall. These crosses were torn down during the Reformation, but many local place names still record their presence. Freewheel down this lane and take the first left. The lane rises and meanders for a few hundred yards before finally exiting onto the main road at the end of **Rue de la Croute**. Turn right here, pass through a crossroads and then fork left into **Rue des Pallieres**.

Miss a left and at the crossroads turn right into **Rue de la Pointe**, heading towards the heathland of Les Landes. Once considered as a site for the island's airport, the only planes that do fly here are model aircraft.

Turn right at the next yellow line and follow the sign on the left towards **Grosnez Castle.**

No visit to St.Ouen would be complete if it did not include Grosnez Castle. Built around 1330, Grosnez is a classic "Bow and Arrow" castle. Unfortunately the lack of a well or any accommodation made it solely a castle of refuge from the constant raids inflicted by the French. It would seem that the castle was taken down stone by stone at the end of the fifteenth century, though the reason why continues to be a mystery.

An example of a latterday stronghold can be seen to the south, where a German artillary observation post sits on the cliff edge. Each slit in the tower would control a separate battery of guns. This is one of seven observation towers unique to the Channel Islands.

Return to the main road, at this yellow line (**D**), we have come 9.79 miles; 15.76 km. Turn right, but exercise some caution as the junction is situated on a blind bend. We pass a small group of houses and three lanes on the left before we meet the heathland again. As we head for the sea, **Rue de la Mare** becomes **Rue du Ouest**. Miss a little lane on the left. The road steepens and once again the full sweep of St. Ouen's Bay can be seen. The rocky outcrops of L'Etacq giving way to the softer textures of Les Mielles.

At the end of **Rue de Ouest** turn right onto **Mont du Vallette**. A glorious freewheel brings us back down to sea level and, passing a lane on the left, the road becomes **Route des Havres**. Continue along Route des Havres, missing two lanes on the left, and take the next right which leads to the slipway. Follow the road left as it skirts the sea wall. After two or three hundred yards, stop and take a look back at the rugged headland of L'Etacq. Remember to bear left a little further on where the road appears to divide. At the yellow line at the end of **La Verte Rue** bear left. Follow the road as it swings to the right, and after passing two roads on the left, we arrive again at the crossroads. Turn right here to return to the start, not forgetting to be careful when crossing at the bend

About the Author

Arthur Lamy was born in Jersey in 1952, and was educated at St. Michael's Preparatory School and Victoria College. He is a third generation Jerseyman, his grandfather having moved to Jersey from Carteret in Normandy just before the turn of the 20th century. After leaving school he spent his first years working as a graphic artist and screen printer.

Though probably best known nowadays as a cycle retailer, Arthur is also a locally and nationally published writer. One of only 15 Jersey people to hold the prestigious Blue Badge tour guiding qualification, Arthur is often found taking visitors and local people on cycle or walking tours around the island. On the odd occasion that his bike is in the garage, Arthur enjoys the company of his wife Sue, and his dog Luke.

More titles from Seaflower Books, all priced at between £4.95 and £9.95 ~

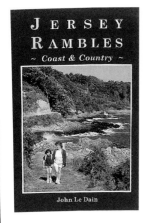

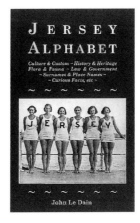

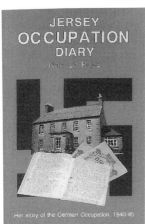

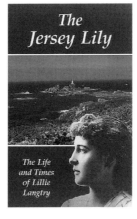

JERSEY HORSES
from the past –

John Jean

JERSEY *in* LONDON

Brian Ahier Read

CHANNEL FISH
A Book of Fish Cookery
from the Channel Islands

Marguerite Paul

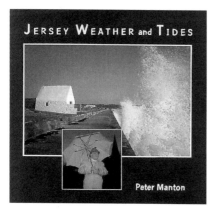

JERSEY WEATHER and TIDES

Peter Manton

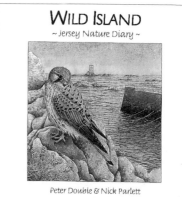

WILD ISLAND
~ *Jersey Nature Diary* ~

Peter Double & Nick Parlett

Guernsey Country Diary

Nigel Jee
Illustrations by Justine Peek

LIFE *on* SARK

Through the year with
Jennifer Cochrane

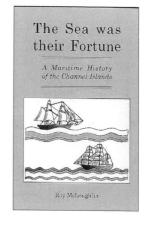

The Sea was
their Fortune

*A Maritime History
of the Channel Islands*

Roy McLoughlin